WALKING CHICAGO'S COAST

WALKING CHICAGO'S COAST

A 63-Mile Journey to the Indiana Dunes

MICHAEL MCCOLLY

NORTHERN ILLINOIS UNIVERSITY PRESS

AN IMPRINT OF

CORNELL UNIVERSITY PRESS

ITHACA AND LONDON

First published 2025 by Cornell University Press

Librarians: A CIP catalog record for this book is available from the Library of Congress.

ISBN 9781501783142 (paperback)
ISBN 9781501783166 (pdf)
ISBN 9781501783159 (epub)

For my mother,
Mickey,
who taught me to walk

Wanderer, your footsteps are
the road, and nothing more;
wanderer, there is no road,
the road is made by walking.

—Antonio Machado

CONTENTS

Illustrations

WALKING CHICAGO'S COAST

I

Beginnings

One knows movement by movement.
—Heraclitus

Rogers Park

The 'L' ascends from under the asphalt aerotropolis of O'Hare and with one glance out the train window, my travels are over. Mile upon mile, the metropolis of the Midwest stretches out before me. The streets and rows of three-flats, the bungalows and corner bars, the brick smokestacks and spires, the peaks of steel and glass, the jagged crown of commerce that lords over the plains, all resting on the buried dead and the remains of an ancient lakebed.

The pale pink sky softens the shock of reentry. I pull my feet up onto the seat, wrap my arms around my knees, and reluctantly let the Chicago Transit Authority reel me the last few miles home. Slumped over and crammed in around me, my fellow Chicagoans sit shoulder to big shoulder. Travelers like me, those of the business class, but mostly those heading home from another long day of selling and serving, stooping and scanning alongside the forty-some thousand other coworkers at O'Hare. Uniformed, IDs hanging from their tired necks, corporate logos on their shirts—the folk that still make this city work. Out the windows, driving fender to fender, filling five lanes on either side of the train, thousands more on the Kennedy creep back into the city or retreat into the rings of suburbia.

Just this morning I'd descended into London's tube station at Charing Cross, a backpack on my shoulders, my legs juiced for another long day of wandering into the hills and along the coastal cliffs of the UK. After three weeks and a couple hundred miles, the land had loosened my hips and strengthened my spine such that to stop walking seemed cruel and self-destructive.

My discontent now, on my return to Chicago, is more than simply the discomforts of jet leg from a transatlantic flight. It's the shock felt by a body that for a time had become freed to follow its inborn instincts and rhythms. There were days walking in the UK where I'd experienced my legs seemingly navigating on their own, energized in a way I'd rarely felt before, bouncing from rock to rock, bounding up ridges.

I'd travelled to the UK to assuage a physical hunger if not a psychological need to feel my body in movement over open landscapes. I'd walked in search of a feeling I'd had in different times in my life while on walks, a feeling I'd first had while wandering the savannahs of Senegal, years ago when working there in the Peace Corps.

Perhaps this sadness that has come over me is the abrupt change in heart rate after days of walking on foot, the decrease in blood flow to the muscles, the diminished use of the organs of perception. Depending on your state of mind and where and how long you walk, there are moments when your body seems to know what the ancient Greeks meant when they coined the word *nostalgia*. We do feel physical pain at the loss of a familiar land beneath our feet. But is it only for a particular place we hold dear because of sentimental value? Or is it that the body itself is disoriented without the feeling of being held by the land—any land?

The L makes its routine stops: Logan Square, Western, Damen, Division and Milwaukee, then sucks me down into the bowels of the Loop and the nexus of the city's transport system. Stumbling through damp concrete tunnels, I navigate myself and my pack up and down two flights of stairs and onto the Red Line bound for Howard. In a blur, the L lifts me up from under the streets and out over the North Side, bounding from Fullerton to Addison to Wilson. And before I know it, I am walking down Sheridan Road past Loyola University and turning east toward the lake at Pratt. Just like that, I'm in my third floor flat, feeling as if I'd gone nowhere. In the past few years, I've begun to feel a heightened sense of anxiety when I return from travel, and particularly from hiking trips—I feel each door closing behind me, each wall sealing me off, each piece of furniture folding me into my proper holding pin. Whether I've spent just a few days in the woodlands of Wisconsin or weeks off in the mountains of Arizona, I feel a sharp twinge of panic once my feet are back on asphalt, the dull dread increasing as I step into a car or bus from having spent several days on foot.

I don't know why I feel this way or why it has increased as I've gotten older. Although I've lived with depression most of my life, that's not what this is; this is more physiological in origin. After my diagnosis with HIV, I wondered at times if the trauma of confronting my mortality was so great that some part of my emotional brain simply broke down. I went about with my life thereafter as best as I could, feigning normality while knowing that my days might be numbered. It was as if to survive, certain emotions necessarily had to be sacrificed. Pleasure and joy were muted. Alone, I found myself often weeping as I watched the local news or read the paper, hearing of some tragedy that had befallen a child or some family. I felt outraged by the insensitivities of others. Often, I berated myself for the slightest mistakes. Grief is a complex emotional state that lingers and manifests itself differently in each of us.

Along with these states of profound melancholia, however, came a strange sense of heightened sensitivity and perception. A veil, it seemed, had been removed from much of the living world. Where before I saw and felt health and promise, I now noticed the inherent fragility in things. I retreated from relationships and found refuge in my work or in intense physical exercise, particularly in natural settings. Here, in the nonhuman world, I felt relief; here perceptions invited states of suspension and imagination.

Basho, the Japanese poet and mendicant monk, describes the wayfarer's desire for wandering as a feeling of being "possessed by the gods," and under this power, he tells us, his soul becomes "turned inside out." Everywhere he looks, the world is calling out to him: "Roadside images seemed to invite me from every corner, so that it was impossible to stay at home."

Perhaps the pain is a signal of distress, a warning that our health is inherently dependent on the land, not just for food and water, but to sustain our abilities to perceive, to learn, to remember, to survive.

Tobey Prinze Beach, Loyola Park

The next day I awaken to the sound of sirens and garbage trucks lifting and dropping metal dumpsters in the alley beneath my window. Dulled by jetlag, my mood worsens when I discover I have no coffee. But whatever ails me or dampens the spirit has a cure and it is only a couple hundred feet out my back door at the end of the alley: the tropical-warm waters of Lake Michigan in late August.

Over the thirty-odd years I've lived in Chicago, I've crept closer and closer to the shores of Lake Michigan. There's nowhere in the city save for a strip on the South Side and here in Rogers Park where someone without a six-figure salary can nestle into a one-bedroom apartment and be able to hear waves breaking on the beaches outside a back window facing an alley. No expressway cuts us off, no skyscrapers block our view, no industrial plants pollute the water or the air that sweeps across this lake.

Out my door, down the steps, and in less time than it takes to make coffee, I am walking barefoot in sand and waving to one of my fellow lake swimmers down the beach, who has just finished her mile-and-a-half-long swim. Here, along Rogers Park's shore, is the only beach directly abutting scores of homes, apartment buildings, and condos. There are palatial million-dollar homes on Lake Michigan further north in the suburbs and around the shore northeast into Michigan, but no community of teachers and workers and taxi drivers has access to Lake Michigan quite like those of us in Rogers Park.

Removed from the hubbub, the high-rises, the crowds and traffic, people flock to this far corner of the city with its intimate public beaches and its thin slice of public space where Loyola Park joins Leone Park. They make pilgrimages on bikes, by foot, by bus or car, as they do along Chicago's formal lakefront. Most are from the surrounding streets and nearby neighborhoods, others come from those landlocked communities to the west, as the beaches along the north shore suburbs require fees and passes for the outsider. Not here.

A Whitmanesque parade to challenge any urban cynic comes and goes all day and late into the evening along this shore. They come to the lake to perform their exercises, their ablutions, their rituals of spirit and community. Wave upon wave of people come, to play, to eat, to sleep, to walk, to sit in silence and stare, reflecting a diversity of need and a diversity of expression nature evokes in us all.

At dawn, all through the year, anglers are already on the end of the pier, a multi-ethnic crowd of mostly men but women, too, with hats and carts full of gear. Then come the beachcombers, gleaners of a sort, picking up bits of flotsam that has floated in overnight. Glass pickers follow, ambling at first but soon bent to scour the surf for their prized chips rolled in from the deep past—Coke bottle blues, 7-Up greens, beer bottle browns. My tribe, the swimmers, breaks the stillness of the lake, arm over arm, out to the buoys along the shore. Next come the children from the Headstart program with their orange bathing caps, blue pails, and yellow plastic shovels. By nine o'clock, free from work and responsibility, the kayakers come, the kite-flyers, board surfers, tight-rope walkers, and the barbecue chefs; alongside these are the working beachgoers: the ice cream man, the lifeguards, and the mothers and their tiny children.

Preachers, ordained and called by the spirit, preachers Black, preachers brown, preachers white, all come to stand in the waves with their reborn, cradling and calling on their God to give them new life. A Thai man once came, and without even turning off his car, ran to the beach, kneeled, placed three sticks of incense into the sand, lit them, said his prayers to the Buddha, and headed back to his car. West African immigrants send their prayers as they chant and shake their fists, entrusting the breaking surf of this great lake named by the Ojibwe to carry their messages to the other world.

This all wouldn't be possible if it hadn't been for determined neighbors led by one Tobey Prinze, a community activist in the early 1960s who wouldn't accept the city's plans to destroy these intimate beaches in order to extend Lake Shore Drive to the northern suburb of Evanston, thereby creating the same barrier that exists for eighteen miles of this famous lake shore. Ingeniously, she got her neighbors to write letters to then-Mayor Richard J. Daley, but they not only included written calls of protests to save their beach—they also sent samples of sand. And it worked.

Plunging into the water, I sense an immediate transformation as my body's buoyancy releases me from the weight, real and imagined, of life on land. For a while the feeling of the water and the warmth of my muscles moving through it eases my mind. I'm content to be aware of just my body swimming along the surface. From the water, the city blurs, its omnipresence diminishes; sounds that define life on shore become static eclipsed by the sudden shriek of a gull or the rhythmic splash of my own arms. What emerges is the land itself, its shape and stature seen from the level of the water: distinct and undefined by what we humans have built upon it.

My mind is free to float along the surface or plunge as it will into memories or fantasies or wonder. Ideas suddenly break through, memories of travel; fantasies find room to unfold. As I've gotten older, lost faces return, forgotten friends and lovers appear, buried sorrows finally find their way out.

Before I know it, I'm past Loyola's campus. Knowing I'll soon begin to lose my stamina from jet lag, I turn back. I scan the lake bottom to keep my depth but mostly for amusement. Sometimes salmon the size of my thigh swivel below, but usually it's sunken trash—the ubiquitous plastic bags, beach toys, bottles, balls, even a naked Barbie doll, once, stretching out her arms as if hoping to be rescued. The washboard effect of the waves on the sandy lakebed triggers a recollection of looking out an airplane window at mountains thousands of feet below in the deserts of the American Southwest. It's strange, an optical illusion. Why would this common feature of the lake bottom, observed countless times before, affect my perception like this? One glance and I am disoriented, momentarily transported to another place and time, making me feel suddenly uneasy.

Is it jetlag? The angle of the sunlight, or the lenses of my goggles? I look down again, believing the effect will disappear. It remains. Is something wrong with my eyes? Something *is* wrong, not with my eyes, but with my mind it seems. I can't unsee the illusion. Panic strikes, then terror with its familiar dread. I stop swimming and tread water.

The shore is a couple hundred feet away. Instead of calming myself, I do the exact opposite. I make a furious push to get myself to shore, swimming and kicking with everything I have. Soon my breath gives out and the panic intensifies. I drop my foot to feel for the lake bottom, but it's still too deep. My exhaustion brings on a sense of anger and disbelief: *This can't be happening to me! Not here! I can't drown in these waters!*

Then, thank God, I remember: *Float!*

Quickly, I turn over on my back and begin to float, bringing my oxygen levels back to normal, calming my nervous system. The panic subsides. I flip back over and do an easy breaststroke toward the shallows, making sure not to look down.

For years I believed that panic attacks were dubious psychological events, experiences that people usually blew out of proportion to draw attention to themselves. Reasonable people didn't have panic attacks, I thought. That was before I found myself drowning in a lake in New Hampshire, exhausted with jetlag after a flight from South Africa. A few months later in a Vietnam hotel I experienced an attack of such potency and dread that I thought I was losing my mind, unable to remember the simplest of words for physical objects such as a chair or a table. A week after that, on a flight bound for Thailand, another attack made me want to climb over people in a desperate attempt to get off the plane. I thought I'd learned my lesson from Pan, the Greek deity of nature who terrorizes the unsuspecting traveler and from which the word *panic* has its origin. Yet, even close to home, panic can strike when we underestimate nature's ability to awaken our respect for its danger and power.

Swimming on, more slowly now, still not looking down, my confidence and rhythm return. Closer to shore, I'm comforted by the recognizable features of the beach I know well. There is a nourishing effect that comes from the basic fabric of places, it seems, the colors and tones of earth and sky, the shapes of trees, the movements of birds, the built environment, those human-made forms we associate with memories of people and the passing of time. Gratefully, I start to think of the mundane duties of my week ahead. Then, seemingly out of nowhere, the idea comes to me: I see myself walking along Chicago's lakefront, far from my apartment. Together, the image and the idea arise in my mind. From here, right on this beach, what prevents me from walking wherever I want to go? From my own apartment doorstep, couldn't I set out and walk all day to the far reaches of this city? There is no reason I can't keep walking as I have the last few weeks in the UK. Couldn't I walk for several days wherever I wanted? Who or what could stop me? The idea is so preposterous but strangely so appealing. I begin to laugh, inhaling a mouthful of water, causing me to choke.

I'd walked along the lakefront path to the Loop training for backpack trips. And I'd taken long night walks through empty streets on my way home from drunken parties. But this would be different. I would be walking to walk, to travel, to explore the very city where I live. I'd be walking where there was nowhere to walk. In effect, I'd be making my own road, bushwhacking beyond the parks and bicycle paths into the edgelands of industrial Chicago and Indiana.

Swimming the rest of the way into shore, I visualize where I'd have to walk, consider the challenges it would entail, think about when I could do it. By the time I get to the shore, I'm convinced I can do it. But I'd have to do it at once, in the next couple of days, or I'd never do it. It was too risky and ridiculous, and I'd talk myself out of it if I thought about it too much.

Walking up through the surf to the beach, I turn back, scanning far over the water to the south and east, to the Indiana shore to see if I can spot the telltale plumes of Gary's steelworks. Further east to Indiana's port and the mill complex at Burns Harbor. And there they are, rising into the hazy horizon, the billowing symbols of smoke that bookend Indiana's dunes. I could do it. In two long days, if I got up early, I could walk around the shore back to Indiana and to those hills of sand where I have so often taken refuge.

Upstairs in my apartment, I pull out a highway map of Chicago, spread it out on a desk and smooth out the folds. I follow the shoreline from Chicago's northern suburbs until the coast curves east along the South Side and cuts a curled chip out of Indiana's rectangular northern border. With my index finger, I trace the shore from my neighborhood, measuring as I go. Each half inch width of my knuckle equals two miles as I inch my way along the map. I count out the mileage along a possible route: Sheridan Road, DuSable Lake Shore Drive, South Shore Boulevard, US 41, Industrial Highway, US 12. Sixty-three miles.

This old map cannot tell me where my path will lead, what I must feel and confront if I attempt such a journey. I will pass through two states and five cities that define this polyglot metropolis of ever-widening social, economic, and environmental divides. I will not be buzzing along at 65 mph on an expressway but rather hiking along truck routes, slinking under tollway bridges, trespassing through corporate property, and navigating forgotten neighborhoods, on foot, alone.

I fold up the map.

But the idea does not go away. All the rest of the day as I go about trying to return to the routines of my life, the idea resurfaces. Later that night, I open my computer and enter into the digitized world as mapped by Google's satellites and its armies of drivers. With a couple of clicks, I discover the precise mileage, see multiple routes, read the names of neighborhoods and cities I will walk through, names now synonymous with America's industrial decline and its environmental and human sacrifices—South Shore, South Chicago, East Side, Hammond, Whiting, East Chicago, and Gary. From Google's satellites, I spot row upon row of white ten-thousand-gallon storage tanks, the unmistakable feature of Northwest Indiana, where petrochemicals are stored and sent out through thousands of miles of pipelines to keep our fuel gauges on full. As my cursor moves over my possible route, I see British Petroleum's gleaming cokers ringed in scaffolding, like missiles on a launching pad. I scan further east and hover over the sprawling marshlands along the Illinois and Indiana border, a watery wilderness of forests, industrial canals, and Waste Management's mountains of trash.

Here are steel mills next to playgrounds, hills of coal along riverbanks, slag piles overtaking sand dunes. Stretches of the shoreline are hidden by the titans of global capitalism—US Steel, British Petroleum, Cleveland Cliffs, Cargill, Unilever, NIPSCO, Union Carbide, and all their many subsidiaries—and the endless sheet metal boxes that house them. I zoom down outside of East Chicago, following a shore I realize I have never seen. A landscape off-limits and well-guarded by security services. Twenty-some miles of America's third coast, a stretch as long as Chicago's lakefront, largely unknown, fenced off, and occupied by nondescript industrial structures and brownfields.

The next day I drive a possible route, through Chicago, then through each of Indiana's industrial cities, hugging the shore, as far as possible and legal. Convincing myself that I won't do it unless I book a room, I pull into the former Trump Casino Hotel in Gary, put down a credit card for a young Black woman at the desk. "Is this for pleasure or business?" she asks, smiling.

"I don't know, I think both."

II

NORTH SIDE

All history is local history.
—JOHN DEWEY

Rogers Park to Hollywood Beach

Two days later, on an unremarkable Tuesday in late August, with temperatures projected in the low 90s, I jump out of bed, the sun already up.

My plan was to begin ceremoniously at sunrise on the beach, head along the shore to Loyola's chapel, Madonna della Strada (Our Lady of the Road),[1] and be on my way. But the night before, I took a deep dive into the internet researching "Superfund Sites in East Chicago," which led me into the troubled environmental history of the "Calumet River," and before I knew it, it was well past midnight.

I throw on my best hiking shorts, dull gray to look as official as I can, opt for the lightest shirt and favorite blue ball hat, carefully smooth out my socks to prevent blisters, and pull on my well-worn, dark gray Salomon hiking shoes. Already late, I rush about, stuff my daypack with a change of clothes, gulp down some food, and unceremoniously exit my apartment. Not halfway down my block, I freeze. Orange street cleaning placards, tied around every other tree, announce that unless I move my car, my urban pilgrimage will cost me sixty bucks.

After circling the streets of my neighborhood, I fit my car into a spot several blocks away. Finally, I'm ready to begin my pilgrimage, but I'm in such a rush that I catch a strap off my pack in the car door and when I take my first step, I tumble back onto the car, then onto the pavement. So, my first step on my journey to Indiana is a humbling pratfall.

Seeing that it's already eight o'clock, I accept that I'll likely walk no further than fifteen miles and then turn around in the city's Loop and go home. So I stop at a CVS drugstore for another power bar and gum. Two blocks later, passing a café I frequent, I give in to the temptation of a coffee and almond croissant. Inside, I scan the tables, half hoping I might recognize someone, which would give me a reason to sit down and abort my pilgrimage altogether. But there's no one who might question my quixotic plan to walk thirty-one miles across Chicago to the outskirts of Gary, Indiana by nightfall.

As I head south on Sheridan Road, high-rise condos line the shore, creating a canyon with apartment buildings on the opposite side. Granville

---

1 Our Lady of The Highway was so named because Loyola University believed when constructing the chapel that the city would eventually extend DuSable Lake Shore Drive. Thus, motorists would be passing before it.

Beach, El Lago, Tiara, Malibu East—the names of these lakeside towers, modern and sleek when first built in the 1960s and 1970s, feign tropical warmth and resort living. But along Sheridan, serene it is not. Buses and delivery trucks stop and start while lanes of traffic jockey aggressively along this notorious bottleneck that feeds North Shore commuters going into and out of the city.

The sidewalks, too, are busy. Students pass, dogs on leashes pull their owners, delivery workers roll carts, joggers run blank-faced among the beachgoers loaded down with bags and chairs. We all share the wide sidewalk here along Sheridan with aplomb, instinctively aware of how to give each other just enough space. No small wonder is the humble sidewalk. So simple in design, these uniform slabs of concrete beneath me, creased to keep them drained. How quintessentially democratic they can be: connecting street to street, block to block, neighborhood to neighborhood, opening the city to all who need them. It's easy to dismiss them until they're not there, or not cleared of snow in winter, or so neglected that they become impassable.

Like the other streets and boulevards, avenues and expressways that cover some fifty-four thousand miles across this city of 225 square miles, these all have names attached to them, historical figures, people whose actions in some way we are asked to remember. Posted below the streetlamp over my head, a green street sign spells it out: Sheridan Road. I have read the name of the Civil War general and legendary figure in Chicago's history, consciously and unconsciously, hundreds of times. But here, today, on foot, at the beginning of this walk, my perception has shifted. By simply telling myself I'm going to walk across the city, there is an awakened sense of the meaning of a simple street sign with a name on it. History comes sprouting up from the very ground—this very road. I'm not walking anywhere today that has not already been walked before by generations of Chicagoans, not to mention those first peoples that settled here along the lake.

Sheridan was the commander of the Missouri, whose troops brought a bloody end to nearly three hundred years of war between the European colonists and Indigenous peoples. When you remember that commanders under him were responsible for the massacres at Sand Creek and Washita River, and that he played a prominent role in the near biocide of the buffalo as a means to starve and demoralize the Sioux, it's hard to look up at this name in green and white and simply shrug away the history. For Chicagoans, Sheridan plays a particular role in the city's tumultuous history, as he not only led the city through the dark days after its devastating fire but also came to the rescue again, leading his troops from the Western frontier on horseback to bring order to the streets after the Haymarket riot shook the city and the country.[2]

Though I doubt Chicago will ever change the name of Sheridan Road, the city did finally recognize its first non-Indigenous resident, Jean Baptist Pointe du Sable, by adding his name to its most famous drive—DuSable Lake Shore Drive.[3] So why not at least rename a part of this famous road for those Indigenous people whose trails became streets here in Chicago?

With my mind untethered to a single purpose, other than to walk and see what happens, the signs remind me that, no matter how far I go, my walk will make me consider the layers of the city's complex history, the one celebrated in statues and street names as well as the history that lives still in the streets and psyches of its people, that history that refuses to be boxed up and buried.

Soon I turn off Sheridan and walk into a shady grove of gingkoes between two high-rise condo towers. There is the vast aqua blue of Lake Michigan and the beginnings of the Lakefront Trail. The path that will take me forward for the next eighteen miles.

---

2 Sheridan's outsized role in the city's history is complex. The general had a home in Chicago and was there the night of the city's conflagration in 1871. His heroic actions that night combatting the fire himself along with soldiers and later his role overseeing the city the days following the fire earned him great respect. However, there's no question of his allegiance to the wealthy barons of the city with whom he socialized and rushed in to protect when labor unrest threatened their power after the Haymarket Affair in 1886. Chicago's streets became a battlefield when a dynamite bomb exploded at the end of a peaceful rally of workers in support of the eight-hour workday. In the ensuing chaos, police opened fire into the crowd. By the time order was restored, eight police and five workers had been killed and many others wounded. Eight anarchists were arrested and charged with conspiracy, and five were publicly hanged, even though none of them had thrown the bomb. The events of the Haymarket Affair sparked protests among organized workers around the world.

3 Though the Pottawatomi had villages and encampments along the shores of Lake Michigan and near the Chicago River inland, the first known permanent non-indigenous resident was Jean Baptist Pointe Pointe du Sable. Du Sable, a Haitian of French and African descent, ran a trading post along with his Pottawatomi wife there at the mouth of the Chicago River, attracting a lively business of both indigenous and French fur traders in the late 18th century.

Hollywood Beach

Though already way off schedule, I cut across Hollywood Beach to the water, taking advantage of the chance to walk on sand. The beach widens as I walk toward Hollywood Pier, technically a breakwater that ties into the beginning of the concrete and limestone revetment wall erected to protect the miles of landscaped park which was built largely on landfill. Ironically, the sand for the beaches here—as elsewhere along Chicago's artificial lakefront—originally came from sand mines along Indiana's and Michigan's shore or was dredged out of the lake.

Except for a few mothers with their children, a clutch of ladies, standing, ankle deep in the water, this wide beach is relatively empty. A pair of swimmers, arms slicing in rhythm, break the placid surface. I watch their smooth progress, heading through the sun's shimmering reflection, brilliant and blinding. What surprising pleasure there is in witnessing the bodies of others moving for the sake of pleasure. Passing the white wooden lifeguard tower with towels and bags hanging on its rungs, I pick up the Polish being spoken by the group of ladies standing in the shallows, arms folded, in flowered suits and caps. I wouldn't normally be so friendly, but I feel compelled to interrupt.

"How's the water?" I call out.

They pause, turning around, wondering if I'm speaking to them.

"Very nice, today. Not too cold."

Like most of Chicago's main beaches, Hollywood Beach is named for the east-west street that feeds into it. Over the years the queer community has staked a claim to a portion of this wide long beach, as its remoteness from the other large beaches further south initially guaranteed less harassment and created an informal public space to meet safely. Now the neighborhoods to the west—Uptown/Andersonville, Edgewater, and mine, Rogers Park—are home to one of the largest LGBTQ communities in the Midwest. By midday this beach will be full of human bodies of every type and age sunning on towels, playing volleyball, lounging, or like these children ahead, immersed in the pleasures of our species' fascination with the magical marginal space where water meets land.

Inland, the warm light illuminates the historic Edgewater Beach Hotel, bringing out its singular soft pink against the blue of the morning city sky.

A reminder of the old shoreline before the construction of the lakefront and DuSable Lake Shore Drive.

Heading toward the breakwater that shields the beach and marks the beginning of the lakefront wall, I recall my recent discovery in the rusting iron girding of Hollywood Pier. How I'd missed it for years on long runs and walks still puzzles me. But one afternoon on a warm fall day, sitting near the pier grading essays, I glanced up from a student's work, and my eye caught what appeared to be a faded string of letters on the rusting pier. Graffiti but barely visible, perhaps spray-painted years ago. There were three letters in a row: an **E**, a **U**, and a **G**. Further, I noticed more: A blurring streak of yellow I couldn't make out. But then, I saw an **N** and maybe an **E**, but I couldn't tell. About a foot further along, there was an **M** and a **C**.

I read the letters without conscious awareness, as the mind absorbs stimuli when we are focused on other subjects, and I went back to reading. But I'd barely read two sentences when my mind had worked out the puzzle on the pier. There had to be more letters. And indeed, there were. Six inches from the **M-C** there was another C and an **A**, followed by an **R**, a **T**, and an **H**. Before I'd found the last **Y**, I got up from the sand and marched to the pier to see for sure. Yes, the yellow blurs were E's spelling **E-U-G-E-N-E**. And following it was **M-C-C-A-R-T-H-Y**. I looked around to find someone to announce my discovery, as if the old anti-war candidate himself was there standing on the pier. Two guys were sitting on towels twenty yards away. Excitedly I began to jog over to them but caught myself. They were too young. They'd not know, they'd just look at me like some lunatic trying to hit on them.

No doubt McCarthy's spray-painted name had survived from that tumultuous summer of 1968 when the city hosted the Democratic National Convention. Here and across the city beaches and parks became both camping grounds and battlegrounds for the throngs of young people who came to Chicago to make their voices heard.

There along the concrete pier, the sand drifting almost to the rusted iron girder, I spot the **E** and the **U** and trace along the other letters with my hand, spelling out the name, still embedded there, of the old senator from Minnesota. Unchanged from the days of the summer of '68, McCarthy's name still evokes the chants, the psychedelic dreams, and the cries from the bloody streets of Chicago.

My mind wanders as I walk up and over Hollywood Pier and onto the tiered revetment wall and walkway that follows the shore. Images come to me of 1968, but not those I saw on television of the police on horseback pursuing protesters or of politicians battling it out on the floor of the convention hall. The image that comes back to me is that of my mother, sisters and me, standing in a small crowd of people on the courthouse steps in my mother's hometown of Gas City, Indiana, her hands folded over her chest listening to Senator Gene McCarthy in his baggy black suit pants, calling on President Johnson to end the war that day in May of 1968. My mother, the small-town activist, wanted my sisters and me to see him, to witness history, to hear what he had to say.

I suppose it isn't really Eugene McCarthy or that summer of 1968 I always think of when I walk along this stretch of the lakefront now, but rather my mother: the social worker, the program director at the YMCA, the special education teacher, the coordinator for the social services hotline for women in Indianapolis, the volunteer who taught men how to read at the state prison, the ever-vigilant fact-checker who'd regularly call in to the radio station to rebut the hysterical fears of members of the

John Birch Society who believed communists were on the school board. My mother the activist, working the phones at the Democratic headquarters, collecting signatures, and going door-to-door to register voters. My mother who, even as she began to lose her memory, went around to the other women locked away like her in the "memory care" wing, reaching for their hands and asking, "Are you okay?"

Her presence here isn't a surprise. When I'm walking along the lakefront, I see her all the time in the bodies of the elderly, the women, arm clutching arm, wobbling as one body, ever so gently along the shore.

Perhaps it is my mother who has inspired this audacious trek. Even as dementia scrambled the maps of her diminishing world, she walked along the beaches and intercoastal riverbanks of northern Florida. "It holds me, this land does," she said once, walking with me along the surf, her outstretched arm and fingers signaling the sand dunes and low flying pelicans over the undulating waves. She held on to her independence until they buckled her into a wheelchair fitted with a loud buzzer to call the nurses if she attempted to take another step. Agency is spirit. And when it is gone, what do we have left?

Hollywood Pier to Foster Beach

I climb up to Hollywood Pier and onto the revetment wall that serves to protect the landfill behind it. This wall is a sort of public stoop where young and old sit or stroll, lounge or stare off into the watery horizon. The city is now slowly rebuilding these walls, creating smooth tiers of concrete for the wheeled world we've become, but I'm still partial to the old limestone boulders, which were fit and stacked and held in by concrete and iron pilings. The "steps" as Chicagoans fondly call them are an architectural landmark as famous as any vertical creation of stone and steel along Michigan Avenue.

To me, the true sculptured artworks of cities are those features of parks and public spaces where we can see and feel the past rubbed into them by those who've made their way before us. These paths of desire as some call them are all around us if we look, and certainly they aren't all made by our feet. By touch, we humans leave our mark.

Out from the cracks in the tiers of worn limestone boulders bloom goldenrod, trees of heaven, and dandelions. And in the rocks themselves, if you look carefully, you can discover the fossil remains of sea creatures, imprints left in the layers of sand of millions of years before.

The cycle of life and love is all played out here from early morning till deep into the night. "WILL YOU MARRY ME?" is a common spray-painted plea along with more desperate cries of "PLEASE DON'T LEAVE ME." Names of lovers tag the whole lakefront; my favorites are those intimately painted in red nail polish. Here couples of every age come to steal away, make out, argue, break up, and get back together. It's also where the lonely linger—to remember or try to forget.

I stop not ten feet from the beginning of the tiered steps, noticing a slab of cut limestone that seems to serve as a kind of perch or table to play chess or dine on. On closer inspection, though, I find that it is a tablet on which someone has etched a passage of poetry.

Here are a series of quotes offered by the philosophical and the inspired, favorite lines of guidance and wisdom. As I stop to read them, traces of a faded inscription come into focus drawn from the stoic mind of Seneca, but I can't make out the passage quoted. Below it, equally worn away by waves and weather, is a line or two from our own American stoic and moralist, Thoreau. But freshly inked for me to read are some lines from Tennyson's "Ulysses":

> Come, my friends, 'tis not too late to seek a newer world.
> Push off, and sitting well in order smite
> The sounding furrows; for my purpose holds
> To sail beyond the sunset, and the baths
> Of all the western stars, until I die.

As romantic as I feel about my adventure across the urban landscape ahead, I'd rather have a hint or kick in the ass from the more somber minds of Thoreau or Seneca, just to keep me honest. Seneca might smile down on me just the same: "It is pleasant at times to play the madman."

But my mood is soon sobered by what I can see just a few yards away: two white tombstones painted on the rocks, one beside the other, as if starting a trend, red letters spelling out "RIP" and, below, "MOM" and her years on earth. These markers always remind me of those I saw painted on the steps a few miles further south near Belmont Harbor, which appeared at the height of the AIDS epidemic. A certain young man named Buck was memorialized there in just the same way, a neat square with just his name and the dates of his coming and going. I'd notice it every time I passed, running or riding my bike or going for a swim, both before I contracted HIV myself in the mid-1990s and after. Once a somber memory of the time when I thought it wasn't possible that I'd be infected, now, when I pass the spot where the marker once was painted some twenty years later, it represents a multitude of stories, places, and people, alive and dead.

Chicagoans personalize their parks as city-dwellers tend to do everywhere, identifying with special corners that become memorable for one reason or another: a tree that they always sit by, a certain bench with a particular view of the lake and the city in the distance, a stretch of beach, a plot of public earth that over time they've come to relate to as if it has called them forth personally to care for and safeguard it. Once after a violent thunderstorm that blew down several large trees near the beach in Rogers Park, I saw a woman visibly shudder and place her hand to her mouth as she saw one of her favorite trees—one of a cluster of languid willows on the beach—split down the middle, its raw orange trunk exposed and splintered. She stood as if struck herself, unable to move, while other neighbors walked around the shattered tree in silence afraid to touch it, like birds and animals do when they mourn their dead.

The revetment wall has become something of a free canvas for people to express themselves, though renovation seems to have curtailed the artwork these days. The lakefront, like city parks everywhere, is also where people gather for public and private rituals, coming out to celebrate the Fourth of July with a million others, as well as those solemn days of winter when you'll see souls searching for something or someone they've come to find, walking alone beside the icy waves and skeletal black oaks.

Ahead, a shirtless white man with a shovel appears to be digging out the overgrown weeds sprouting from the cracks. I stop and offer my amazement at his civic pride, but he laughs it off: "Why not? It's my exercise. I see my neighbors. It's sunny. I come out, do a little work. Go home. I did it last year, too. It took half the summer, but I got all the way to Foster Beach."

"Has anyone from the city thanked you?"

"Are you kidding?" He chuckles, rolling both his eyes and his head, as he goes back to work, his shovel scrapping against the stone.

I make my way to the end of the wall and am about to step back on the sand at Foster Beach when I spot someone else on a self-assigned mission, an older white man I see out here often on my walks. He's curious looking, with a floppy camouflage hat, shorts, and well-worn tennis shoes. He carries two plastic bags in each hand with another tied to his belt, fastidiously collecting and stuffing trash into them as he scurries from Starbucks cup to aluminum can to errant plastic bag.

I stop and ask this familiar fixture of Hollywood Beach why I always see him out here picking up the trash. "I live over there," he tells me, pointing nervously at one of the high-rises behind us back at Hollywood Beach. "I've come out here for twenty years. And now, I go to Foster, too." He points to the beach up ahead. "I don't want any praise," he says as he sees my camera. "I don't want any attention, please."

I've interrupted his morning ritual, his meditative work. He fidgets and looks about, but then, as I bow and begin to depart, out comes his story. "One day I was out here with my daughter, and she'd stepped on a piece of glass, a bad cut that needed stitching." He points back to where I've been walking, recalling this episode as if it had happened only yesterday. "The glass, it's everywhere," he says, his hand sweeping from south to north along the lakefront. "I just hope that maybe I can prevent an accident. Like what happened to my daughter," he sighs, shaking his head, his body seemingly sinking with the thought of his impossible but necessary duty. "There's so much out here."

The trash man made me think of the many gleaners I've seen for years all along the lakeshore from the beaches of Chicago to where I'm headed, the Indiana Dunes. They sort out what might be useful and scour the shore for shards that have been tumbled and polished by the waves into what is called "lake glass." On days when I find myself without purpose, meandering about my rooms in a fog of depression, I force myself into the sunlight and become part of this tribe of beachcombers, too. I've learned that a half-hour of stooping and fingering the scraps from the surf can redirect my emotions and perhaps offer me a talisman of good fortune to add to my rather large collection of stones, bricks, gnarled knots of driftwood, and my favorites—fishing lures faded from years in the water.

There are the professionals—the men with the metal detectors, sweeping over the beach and shallows, scrounging for someone's loss. And there are the glass-pickers, almost all women, their backs bent, their plastic bags full of smooth colored glass from which they make jewelry or knick-knacks. When I swim, I frequently run into a Black woman who walks with a cane in the tumbling surf, searching for what she calls her "lake gems." "I use them to make my prayer jars," she told me once. "I like to give them to my friends." She has metal braces on both her legs, and though it looks like her cane is used to steady her, it's more of a tool to sift through the sand and stones rolling over her bare feet. The cane, too, often serves as a hand as she waves to her friends—others like her, who have found their reasons to meander on the margins between lake and city.

Before me now are more faded canvasses on the rock and concrete: a giant hand painted with Hindu sacred symbols, psychedelic swirls and flowers, rainbows, Mayan deities, cartoon characters, a US flag that appeared around the time of 9/11 as I recall, and of course plenty of hearts.

Crossing back to the beach, I think of the trash man and his worry about glass as I catch myself looking more carefully at the flotsam and bits of garbage at my feet, the plastic residue of our consumer culture: the bottle caps and dead balloons, the bags and bits of broken beach toys. My gaze has shifted, my eyes are freed to see what's here—not as I've seen it before, but as a pilgrim might on a road where anything and everything could have significance.

Foster Beach to Montrose Point

After tromping along the shore at Foster Beach, I climb back up onto the revetment wall, side-step a few picnickers stretching out in the grass overlooking the lake, and head toward Montrose Point. Instead of following the main Lakefront Trail, I stay along the shore to take in the longest, largest, and probably most well-used beach along Chicago's shore, Montrose Beach.

It must be past nine o'clock and the park lands here are filling up even for a Tuesday—Latino families are setting up for the day with chairs and grills, joggers in groups out for their daily runs. There's a soccer match or two—one for girls with their parents crowding the pitch, another with men from what looks like a dozen nationalities dribbling and defending in the open field of artificial grass.

By and large people come to the lakefront in groups: families gathering with relatives for birthdays and cookouts; players to meet their teammates for sport; joggers in twos and threes to take their runs; dads and moms with their children to play in the sand and swim; couples on dates; even the dog owners have their pets who themselves need exercise and sociability. I notice this not because I'm on a mission to walk the lakefront but because I'm a single man. Almost everywhere I go I'm conscious of the difference between those like me who are alone and those who are in pairs and groups.

Of the many challenges ahead of me—the fatigue, the heat, the blisters, the cars and trucks, the dangers of wandering in unfamiliar neighborhoods—there's also that age-old sadness I've known almost since I moved to Chicago four decades ago: the feeling of being alone in the convivial crowds of parkgoers. It's there like the clothing I wear, clothing that I can't take off, that says to anyone who notices, "He's alone." When I am swimming, far from shore, the water seems to wash the loneliness away, but back on shore it's always there.

Today I tell myself I'm immune to that feeling. I have an identity, like I do when I swim. I'm like the man picking up trash, the beachcombers, the solitary birders—I have a purpose. I'm walking the lakefront, I'm a pilgrim on a quest across the city.

Over the years, the far south end of Montrose Beach and the tip of Montrose Harbor have become something of a refuge for me and many others who've discovered and participated in the rewilding of this corner of Chicago's coast. When the weather breaks and the psychological gloom of urban winter lifts, I push myself out of my cage and head south almost unconsciously to Montrose Beach. Like the migrating birds and butterflies, people too flock to this thirteen-acre patch of rewilding nature.

It's common to call these corners "escapes," where one can feel outside of the city while being in it. But aren't these places we discover in cities more like portals into where we are and live? This idea of escape unnecessarily divides a world that nowhere is truly divided. Maybe this walking through the city is an act of touching and sensing the world as undivided.

Discovering the wilds within this city is nothing new. Leonard Dubkin, a Chicago naturalist and writer, for years wrote a popular column and several books about the city's natural world. Be it backyards, weedy lots, or the banks of the Chicago River, Dubkin opened up the wilds of the urban landscapes for his readers, sharing with them his walks, his adventures into the parks and alleys and odd corners of the city, and the creatures—human and nonhuman—that inhabited them. Indeed, I'm trying to follow his sage advice in this walk: "It seems to me that people are forever traveling great distances, and journeying to strange countries, to see things that, if they only knew it, exist beside their own doorsteps."

To the uninformed eye this somewhat remote section of the beach looks unsightly, neglected by the normally fastidious Park District. Indeed, there isn't a clean sandy beach here or a tidy lawn with shady maples and oaks for picnickers to enjoy views of the lake and the city's magnificent skyline to the south. If you came here not long ago, you'd have seen trash swirling around in the corners by the long fishing pier, and above the beach high stands of weeds, a few trees, a hedge of honeysuckle and brambles along the inner drive that leads to the marina.

What has happened here accidentally or providentially challenges traditional ideas of urban park space. The rewilding of Montrose began in

the Cold War era, when fears of Russian attacks led to amped-up efforts to guard America's large industrial cities on the coasts and on its inland seas as well. Montrose was selected for a Nike missile site, like many other places strategically positioned across the Great Lakes. When the scare died down, the US Army broke down the barracks and shipped out, leaving trees and a hedge of honeysuckle planted by the men stationed there, who apparently noticed that though the Russians never bothered to show, flocks of migrating birds did, gravitating, for shelter and rest, to the honeysuckle and shrubbery.

The Lake Michigan shoreline acts as a funnel for one of the largest bird migration routes in the world, as it has for thousands of years. It requires an effort of the imagination to recall that most of metropolitan Chicago and hundreds of square miles extending south into Indiana and northern Illinois constituted part of a massive flood plain of marshes and wet prairie as large as the Everglades before settlers drained it at an astonishing rate in the late nineteenth century. The drainage of Lake Michigan's flood plain is estimated to have reduced America's migratory bird population by twenty percent by the beginning of the twentieth century.

After the military broke camp at Montrose Harbor in the mid 1970s, the area reverted to park space, but it wasn't well maintained and was frequented only by those who fished off the long concrete breaker that protected the beach. Beachgoers and picnickers generally stayed away; winds swept trash to the far end of the beach and erosion began to unveil the unsightly landfill rubble that lay beneath the grassy parks and beaches. Little used, the park above this corner of the beach became overgrown with thickets and weeds. As with all edgelands and marginal zones in urban areas, it attracted the marginalized as well—rebellious teens, drug users, and men looking for hookups with other men. And so, it remained. For the bird population, the growth of trees, weeds, native grasses, and brambles created a more hospitable habitat. The spontaneous rewilding of Montrose had begun.

But the story of the rewilding of Montrose doesn't end there. In winter, here as elsewhere along the lake, the winds and waves reshape the beaches as sands are added or eroded. By May, when the crowds begin to emerge from their winter hibernation, the park district starts to rake and groom the beaches. In some spots, grasses, reeds, and cottonwood saplings have taken root. Most places, the city tractors plow the budding growth under along with sandals, plastic bags, aluminum cans, and whatever else has washed up on shore over the winter. But at Montrose, the beach is long, and over time, park district groundskeepers began to let part of the south end go, thinking because the area was unpopular it wouldn't matter much.

But it did. After a year of little maintenance, beachgoers noticed that stands of marram grass, traditional dune-builders, had taken firm grip on several sections. Around them small piles of sand had formed. Along the pier as well, water had pooled in an eroded spot and wind had further created marshy zones where shoots of sedge appeared, along with reeds and other indigenous plants that for centuries had dominated the entire southern end of Lake Michigan. Among the clumps of grasses, up popped that other sturdy dune-builder, the ubiquitous and ever-ready-to-root cottonwood, its heart-shaped leaves quivering in the lake breezes. The birders in the bushes and grasses above began to take note of the increase in species on the shore. Along with the usual sightings of shore birds found along the lakefront, now birders flock to see rare and uncommon species that frequent this corner of the lakefront. Here, where the Audubon Society reports the sighting of over three hundred species, one can spot snowy owls and short-eared owls, loons, warblers, and peregrine falcons, and now even piping plovers nest on the restored beaches.

It's out of the way to walk out to this strip of wilderness, but what's the point of this walk if not to saunter through those parts of the city and the lakefront that over the years have given me pleasure?

I volunteered here at Montrose on and off a few years ago, picking up trash, helping to plant native trees, removing invasive species, watering. The work led me to projects conserving beach landscapes further north on the beaches near me in Rogers Park. Here, there's a memory of those quiet mornings fingering plants that grounded me, gave me physical and emotional rootedness.

Walking in the foredunes that have emerged here where sand has mounded around cottonwoods that naturally seeded themselves, I see the black oaks I helped water and plant. Passing them, I notice their growth. I make a point to stop and assess their progress, often grabbing their trunk with my hands, and just holding it there to feel them, know they're alive. Touching is such a simple act. Nothing gives you more of a sense of belonging to a place than planting and caring for trees.

In fact, I often make pilgrimages like I'm doing today, though I don't consciously set out thinking that's why I'm walking to Montrose or to the trees I've planted. But when I arrive, I know why I am there. For people like me without children, a tree—one single tree—can offer something that might be similar to a parental sensibility; touching them awakens a certain instinct that I can't know unless I'm near them.

I slog through the sand to the southern tip. I see others like me, solitary birders meandering on the trails that I've mulched and weeded. Some carry their telescopic lenses, some stroll and stop and stare, some hold out their hands with nuts and seeds hoping to entice a chickadee to feed.

Above the restored dunal landscape and maturing swale with its reeds, the cardinals call and nearby red-winged blackbirds sing out their plaintive song, *conk la reee!* Though I carry binoculars, I don't need them. I've learned that part of birdwatching is more than just feeling the excitement of seeing an uncommon species. It's actually staying present with a bird so that I can feel that I'm being seen in return—in the blackbird song, so common as it rings in my ear, *conk la reee!*, I hear all the places in which these birds have called out to me.

And so, as I walk up through the bird sanctuary and down onto the beach, for a while I forget where I am heading and think instead about what I have witnessed here over the last couple of decades. I'm aware of how nature and a collective vision of citizens—not park officials or landscape architects or wealthy donors—have reshaped this corner of the lakefront. Scanning this undulating habitat with its small dunes capped with maturing cottonwoods, its stands of willow, its clumps of tall grasses, and its thick carpet of sedges and reeds that cover what was once a man-made beach, I see the past and the future, the city not as separate but as a part of the ongoing flowering of this landscape along Lake Michigan.

Montrose Harbor to Diversey Harbor

The Lakefront Trail is a roughly fifteen-foot-wide asphalt path with crushed limestone on either side. It'll be, if I make it that far, my route until it ends on the far South Side, some sixteen more miles. Circling around Montrose Harbor, I head into the heavily used section of the trail in Lincoln Park. Depending upon the time of day, the trail can look as congested as DuSable Lake Shore Drive, which in some places is only a few feet away. Cycling commuters, joggers, ambling tourists, dog walkers, parents running with strollers, ice cream salesmen, triathletes, and maybe even a few bona fide hikers share this exercise expressway along the shore.

From time to time on long walks, I've experimented with various techniques I've gleaned from years of dabbling in meditative practices from the East. Perhaps, I should consider the methods of meditative monks rather than athletes. A few years earlier, I'd spent some time in a Buddhist monastery in northern Thailand, which meant rising at dawn and spending all day alternating between sitting and walking meditation. No leaving the grounds, no food past noon, no reading, no exercising, no talking to the monks. As anyone who has devoted themselves to the rigors of such practices knows, it's not the body that rebels under sustained efforts of discipline, but the mind. I got the hang of slowing down to a snail's pace by finally paying attention to the elderly Thai widows, watching them in their long shawls gliding over the old cobblestone temple plaza under the moonlight. I learned to sense the subtle workings of the core muscles that balance the weight of the body with each slow step. But after a week, under the rules and strict schedule of the monks, I couldn't take another hour of battling my adolescent mind and admitted defeat.

In the end, whether one is hiking up a steep mountain or walking slowly step by step in a monastery, essentially, it all does come down to putting one foot in front of the other.

For a while on my path here in Lincoln Park, I try to remember the techniques of my elderly Thai teachers and pay close attention to the proprioception of my body as it walks: the knees bending, the legs lifting, the toes touching, the heels rolling through. But in no time, I'm back to the basics that our ancestors worked out thousands of generations ago: lift, step, push off, catch the body just as it begins to fall with the other foot, and repeat until no mental effort is required to continue. Not quite the mythic perfection of the perpetual motion machine but not bad for a two-legged animal that once had to compete with others to survive on the African savannah.

I stay close to the lake, making my way around the backside of Waveland Golf Course. Wincing with each thwack of metal on rubber—knowing from experience the potential unintended consequences of the golfer's slice—I cross back to the trail, skirting around the outfield of a baseball diamond where two teams of women are playing softball.

My mind is unmoored, not sure of where to focus. I catch myself glancing at an architectural feature on the top of a building or some such novelty I've never noticed before, but then a few minutes later my mind slips back; my eyes only see what is familiar, and everything becomes the usual blurry background to my cycling thoughts and emotions.

Why is it so difficult to stay absorbed and see what appears as I walk without the endless reverb, that obsessive need to analyze? Why can't I just enjoy it for what it is? I remember my mother in her Alzheimer's-affected mind and shrinking little body and voice, sitting there in her wheelchair and asking with such clarity and concern for me, "Oh, honey, let's enjoy the enjoying, okay?"

Entering Lincoln Park, which merges with the lakefront, I come upon a forty-foot totem pole, a replica of the original gifted to the city by the Kwakiutl people of Vancouver Island in British Columbia, recreated with generous support from the cheese magnate and founder of Kraft Foods, James Kraft. Though it's as much a fixture of the city and Lincoln Park as the lions in front of the Art Institute of Chicago, for me, despite its aesthetic quality and attempt to honor a group of peoples of North America, it seems awkwardly out of place.

What's not to admire about a dramatic piece of public sculpture like this, nestled between the tennis courts and the Belmont Harbor Yacht Club? I stop and look at it, as I often do. The specific stories and powers of the boldly carved and painted mythological creatures are artfully evoked by the totem pole's sculptor, Tony Hunt. By the time your eye reaches the Thunderbird perched on the top, painted in gold, green, and red, your imagination has been primed by the other figures that hold it aloft: a mythical sea monster and a human riding a humpback whale. For Chicagoans, the totem pole "Kwa-Ma-Rolas" (the Thunderbird) is a reminder of the city's past. Its original was in Chicago's Columbian Exhibition of 1893, part of a living diorama where Indigenous peoples from all over North America exhibited their ways of life to the fairgoers. But you would not know this by glancing at the modern replica. Here, there's little to learn about the cultural significance of the totem pole or of this one in particular.[4]

---

4 At the Field Museum you can find other totem poles once a part of the American Indigenous people's exhibition at the Chicago World's Fair. There, you can learn about Kwakiutl history and culture; admire the craftsmanship of their boats, their artistry in shaping tools and fishing hooks, and their sacred masks; and learn something of the power and ancestral reverence of totem poles.

Up ahead, between Belmont Harbor and Diversey Harbor, there are a couple more monuments dedicated to Indigenous peoples. As I pass the stately bronze Ottawa warrior and his family, entitled "Alert," and then, a bit further along, the rather forlorn depiction of a Sioux chief on his horse called "Signal of Peace," I stop and study them. For thirty years, riding by on a bike or looking out of the window of a bus, I've noticed them, like dozens of public memorials or pieces of public art in and around the city. I wonder: what purpose do they really serve? Is this statue of a forlorn and dejected chief sitting on his horse with a flag signaling peace (or surrender?) really what the Sioux themselves would erect to honor their ancestors and their fierce spirit in battle to uphold their culture? Parks are full of these antiquated and dishonest depictions of American history. Chicago certainly doesn't have a monopoly on that. We walk and drive by them every day. They go unseen, accepted as versions of history, until we stop and question why, as we learn more about the past, they seem to remain. Along the lakefront, where so many heroes, including Sheridan, are honored, it would seem appropriate to give space to those peoples whose ancestors remain in the region—for example, the Potawatomi, or other tribes of the upper Midwest. Where is the statue to Blackhawk? To Tecumseh? How about a monument to Jean-Baptist du Sable's spouse, a Potawatomi? Where are the depictions of what happened, actually happened, here?

Of course there are all kinds of public art works, plaques, and statues erected around the city, especially here on the lakefront, that we barely take notice of. But today, because I'm on the ground and have the time to contemplate them, I can't help but see those that reflect dated beliefs and historical injustice.

Lincoln Park

Somewhere along this trail is where I first experienced urban jogging back when I moved to Chicago in 1980 to try my hand at acting. As it has been for generations, Chicago is still the destination for small-town dreamers, not just from the American Midwest but also from halfway around the world, who come hoping for fortune, love, and new identities but often find themselves like the tragic characters that so many of the city's writers have immortalized in their fiction and ballads, from Theodore Dreiser's Sister Carrie to Richard Wright's Bigger Thomas. This city has never had a shortage of innocent souls to exploit. My acting career ended before it ever began, as is the case with most of us from places smaller than our dreams. Broke, living in a friend's studio closet in the nearby Lakeview neighborhood, I spent those early days in this city sitting for hours, reading and writing at the libraries, visiting the zoo and the museums on the free days, but mostly walking briskly down Broadway, pretending I had someplace to go.

But on the lakefront, during those first months in the big city, I felt free from the loneliness and torment. As I walk now, I recall how my youthful body felt when I first ran along the lakefront, joining that new breed of urban outdoor enthusiast: the jogger. The lake and the sky buoyed me along, lifting my spirits and legs, and I remember sometimes I'd run miles all the way to the Loop and it would take me forever to walk back to my apartment, as I was so often carried away by the feeling that here, at least, I belonged, even if I had few friends and no money.

I've been through this portion of the lakefront scores of times, albeit mostly on a bike, and rarely think about those months when I first lived here before shipping out to West Africa to join the Peace Corps. As I head on down the gravel path toward the towers of the Loop, I wonder why these memories are resurfacing with such clarity. Is it because my mind has the time to entertain them? Or is it the land itself and the built environment upon it, revealing that though I rarely pay attention to them, they have held on to me?

At Diversey Harbor, Lincoln Park widens considerably to the west on the other side of DuSable Lake Shore Drive. Outside of the lakefront, Lincoln Park is Chicago's largest and most heavily used park with all the classic elements and landscape features of European parks: lagoons, formal gardens, groves of trees, meadows, promenades, statuary honoring heroes and literary icons, museums, a conservatory, and the centerpiece— a zoological garden.

Someone flying by on a bike calls out my name, but by the time I look up they've ridden on. A student, no doubt. After years of teaching writing at half a dozen colleges in Chicago, I see students pop out of the cityscape to remind me of what role I might have played in their lives, particularly the immigrants I taught in ESL classes. At a stoplight, a guy driving an ambulance will roll down his window and ask me on my bike, "Didn't you teach at Northeastern?" A Latina mother, with two tiny children holding onto her coat, will pull on my backpack at a street fair: "You were my teacher at Roosevelt, weren't you?" On the train, students come up to me, dressed for downtown jobs, proudly sticking out their hands, "Mister McColly, remember me?" I don't remember their names, but their voices bring back those scenes in college classrooms, bring back those stories they wrote in journals, stories of struggle, stories of crossing deserts and oceans, climbing mountains, carrying siblings, running from men with guns. Seeing my former students brings back, too, those days I stood before them, dizzy from the HIV drugs I had to take that made my face burn and my hands shaky. One chance encounter on the street can also evoke memories of the warm faces of those students who'd come up to me after class to ask, "Is something wrong?"

Heading toward the Fullerton Avenue underpass that leads directly into the park and the upscale neighborhood further west of the same name, I walk under a familiar stand of black oaks. The tiered steps of stone that once defined this curving section of the lakefront have now been uniformly covered with wide, smooth terraces of concrete. But I still see the exposed iron pilings, the uneven blocks of limestone, and the fissures between them where keys, rings, toys, and tennis balls have been lodged or lost. The shadows of the oak trees, the traffic, the fishermen along the inlet to Diversey Harbor—all conspire to recreate the contours of those days in the nineties when I came here to swim and play with my dog, JD.

Two or three times a week in the warmer months, she brought me here to the lake's edge to keep me from retreating from a world I no longer believed offered a future. Repeatedly, robotically, I threw a slimy, lime-green tennis ball into the lake for her to fetch. Out she swam, no matter the surf, tirelessly, jumping off those crumbling blocks of limestone, determined to please. Part beagle, part pointer, part mutt, white with tan spots, she came up to just shy of my knee. She had been bred for hunting in the wooded hill country of southern Indiana, where my sister picked her out from a neighbor's kennel, convinced a dog would do me good.

Gregarious to a fault, she greeted all friendly dogs regardless of size or owner, and anyone and everyone who passed us by, especially small children and people who didn't want to be bothered, dragging me into encounters no matter my mood. Dogs instinctively demand that we as animals must follow their lead and, following the sound advice of the Roman poet Horace, "seize the day!"

I'd take her out to toss that filthy tennis ball, again and again. When the water wasn't too choppy, I'd tie her leash around a pole and swim out afterward. I'd attempted the first time to see if she'd stay, but when I was halfway out, there she came, paddling furiously to catch me, up and over the waves. I turned back for her, trying to lead her back, but she clawed and scraped my arms and stomach, desperate not for my help but to help me. Bleeding, we made it back. How loyal that dog was. Her memory sticks by me as fiercely as she did that night when she lay there after I took my first dose of AZT, which caused such an adverse reaction that I fainted after getting up to go the bathroom and found myself on the floor.

As the Lakefront Trail curves around the old brick field house at Fullerton Avenue, here she is on the lakefront with me again, her shadow swimming out there in the rough surf, paddling away, trying to keep up with me as I swim out. She'd seen me through the darkest patches of my life before and after my diagnosis, watching over me, sleeping at the foot of my bed, pushing me out, day after day, demanding that I re-engage with the world and its embrace.

After I had to ask my sister to take her back to southern Indiana, for months dog owners that knew me by my dog but not by name came up to me and asked, "Where's that dog of yours?" I told them, and myself, that my traveling made it impossible for me to keep her. I'd hoped to take her back. But she ran away, and my sister feared she'd been killed by coyotes.

It took a long time before I stopped dreaming of her and seeing her in the park out of the corner of my eye or here along the Lake.

Passing Fullerton, the lakefront narrows to essentially a concrete boardwalk and a thin strip of beach punctuated every thirty yards or so by eroding concrete breakers. There is a short clip of footage I came across once on a late-night excursion through YouTube, where Allen Ginsberg and a circle of hippies sit on a beach chanting to Shiva. I had to play it over three times before I realized that the surf, breaking behind them and holding their rhythm, wasn't that of the Pacific or the Atlantic but rather of Lake Michigan. The hippies had followed Ginsberg from Lincoln Park to sit by the lake and chant for peace that infamous summer of 1968. Lincoln Park served as a kind of commons, as public spaces often do organically. Everyone remembers the bloody battles in Grant Park, but here in Lincoln Park, protesters gathered, played music, listened to the impassioned speakers and the poetry of Robert Lowell, Allen Ginsberg, and others. But despite the poetry and music and the pleas of Abbie Hoffman ("We're just here to be with the animals"), the Chicago police forced them out with tear gas and batons.

The area that is now the southeastern section of Lincoln Park was originally outside the city limits. Here, the land was much like the original shoreline: windswept dunes, dunal ponds, marshes, even unstable sand pits, as well as intermittent groves of black oak and cottonwood. Prior to the Civil War, the city erected a cholera hospital here and hastily buried the hundreds who succumbed to the pernicious disease, along with smallpox victims and scores of Confederate prisoners. Residents nearby, never happy with either the hospital or the buried diseased bodies, had already been calling on the city to move the cemetery and convert the area into a park to accommodate the growing city. When storms blew in and exposed some of the graves, public officials believed the cemetery posed a health hazard. Ultimately, the city's battle with cholera would only be truly ended with the reversal of the Chicago River, directing its flow into the Sanitary and Ship Canal, which fed the city's sewage westward toward the Des Plaines River, rather than allowing it to mingle with the city's drinking water in Lake Michigan.

The last time I visited Lincoln Park's Zoo was not to see any of the actual animals enclosed within their cages but rather to observe the annual spring nesting of the reclusive black-crowned night herons. These birds have taken a liking to the tall oaks surrounding a paddle boat lagoon next to the very popular petting zoo and outdoor café. Remarkably, the herons, endangered in much of the US, seem quite content to nest in growing numbers here in Lincoln Park.

For years, I never bothered to go birdwatching in the city, preferring to leave and go to the Indiana Dunes or other nearby marshes or forests outside the city, even though Chicago's shore during spring and fall can be thick with migrating passerines and waterfowl. Birdwatching in cities depressed me somehow. I needed to feel removed from the human-dominated skies. Birdwatching was sitting atop one of Indiana's dunes watching migrating raptors floating on eddies of wind over the lake. It was kayaking down the Chicago River and floating fifteen feet from a hunching green heron blending into the woody bank. Birdwatching was encountering what was left of what was once wild in me.

But as I've aged, I've become either more desperate or more grateful for whatever bird happens to catch my eye. I see the hawks on the wires along the highways and in the dead branches of the sycamore. I take note of the crows sounding off from treetop to treetop in the park, wishing I understood their language. I spot the unmistakable blood-red feathers of a dead ruby-crowned kinglet on the sidewalk in the Loop, fallen from flying into a sheet of glass many floors above. Living near the lake, I have found in birds what my dog once was for me—a reconnection to the living world around me. In them I recognize the ephemeral nature of life, in their vulnerability I feel my own. For what is fate to the kingbird or the robin? They weather the winter storms with resilience. They survive despite our stupidity, possessing a will to make do with the world as they find it.

Birds and wild animals provide fleeting moments of observation that come unannounced, which can release us from those spells that dim the spirit for days on end. I've noticed that the more you stop and look, the more creatures you will see that share the streets and the spaces we all inhabit. They become like living landmarks, cairns, keeping you from losing your way.

I've spent hours staring out my apartment windows at the sparrows on my little enclosed wooden three-flat porch. I've seen mourning doves mate, rubbing their beaks as if kissing. I've seen them build nests in storms in hanging pots and push their young out into the world of flight. I've also seen an attacking kestrel trap and splatter a sparrow's blood on newly fallen snow, shocking me so that I broke out into childlike laughter and jumped around my apartment for reasons I don't understand. Red-tailed hawks have perched on the rail of my back steps and ripped open the remains of small mammals they've caught in the alley. I once had to rescue a tiny old white poodle from a swooping peregrine falcon on my neighborhood beach, tackling the poor creature to protect it, but causing alarm to the oblivious owner who was sure I was a lunatic.

"What did you do *that* for! You scared my dog!"

"Lady, didn't you see the falcon trying to pick up your dog?"

"What? A bird? Attacking my dog?"

And with that she grabbed her poodle, pulled the shaggy mop to her chest, and walked off in a huff.

At other moments, I've stood in the middle of a sidewalk listening to a purple finch or a magnolia warbler and without binoculars tried to point it out to a neighbor passing by, taking the liberty in my enthusiasm of putting my hands on their heads to direct their gaze: "See it? There, there where my finger's pointing?" And when they do see, their mouths hang open like children's, and they exclaim, "Oh my god, is that someone's parakeet? We really have birds like that here?" Then they turn to me for a moment and we both nod to one another before going on with our day.

Like my father did when we traveled cross-country, I call out the red-tailed hawks and the kestrels on the fence posts and dead branches over the highway. I've nearly caused accidents, too. Once, I walked out of a Jewel grocery and was stopped in my tracks in the middle of a parking lot by the unmistakable squawking sound of migrating sandhill cranes floating high over the city. Leaning my head back, I followed them, forgetting that I was standing in an exit lane until someone politely honked, looking at me as if I'd lost my mind, which in a way I had. A screech in the night, a loon's quivering call echoing over a lake, a howl over the hill—all are voices, echoes from another age, before language separated us from the creatures that we learned to mimic and follow.

North Avenue Beach to Navy Pier

After passing the throngs of bathers at North Avenue Beach, the Lakefront Trail intersects the concrete boardwalk that follows the North Avenue Pier and one of the few pedestrian tunnels under DuSable Lake Shore Drive, which shoots a steady stream of cyclists, joggers, and beachgoers onto the lakefront. But as busy as the junction can be, with bodies coming and going and buses and traffic speeding by only yards away, this shady corner exudes a sense of calm.

Stopping to take a drink at a water fountain along the trail, I look around me, wondering again what it is about this patch of artificial land that has absorbed me all these years. Surely it has to do with the grove of trees planted years before—oaks and maples and later crab apple trees—that now protect the pavilion where people have always come to play chess.

The chess players here are almost all older Black men, though their challengers are as diverse as the city. You can't help but be slowed down and pulled into their concentration as they sit contemplating their next moves, pipes locked into the corners of their mouths, meditative fingers hovering over a rook until, with a flourish, a piece is removed and the timer is tapped. I feel compelled to follow their eyes to find out what has inspired their focus, just as I do with the landscape painters who set up their easels all along this shore. Even though I'm trying to hurry along, I find myself shifting my eyes away from the expanse of the lake and over to a huddled group of onlookers watching the play of another older gentlemen and his opponent, a blond-haired youngster barely able to touch his feet to the ground, as they hunch over the black-and-white-checkered board inlaid into the stone bench between them.

Below the chess players, there is a concrete boardwalk, ten yards wide, pitched toward the water to keep crashing waves from spraying and flooding onto DuSable Lake Shore Drive during storms. From this junction

at North Avenue, the trail becomes concrete again, and the only barrier separating its cyclists, pedestrians, and runners from traffic is a short concrete wall and an aging chain-link fence. One distracted cell phone user's mistake could bring a spinning SUV plowing into me and twenty other unsuspecting bodies. Some see the Drive as a symbol of the city, and this stretch to my right finds its way into almost every movie made in Chicago: that quintessential scene of city and lake as seen from a sleek car gliding along a band of asphalt toward the Drake Hotel with the John Hancock Center towering behind it. But if I had my way, I'd bring lake and city back together by burying this outdated monument to the auto and banishing its boxes of metal to a tunnel.

Old photos of this stretch of the lakefront before the construction of Lake Shore Drive reveal why Chicago became such a showcase for modern architecture. The horizontal line of the lake not only emphasizes these towering vertical forms so synonymous with the city but also creates a dazzling double mirrored in the water that changes by the hour as the sun rises and sets. Here, the artificial and elemental come together, one revealing the aesthetic miracle of the other. From a hundred feet out in the water, swimming along this stretch, it seems as if you're flying as each building floats along beside you. Fat chance Chicago would ever consider such a radical and expensive make-over as burying DuSable Lake Shore Drive—but recall the words of the city's famed architect and urban planner Daniel Burnham, whose Plan of Chicago left the city with its de facto motto: "Make no little plans. They have no magic to stir men's blood." It's worth quoting Burnham's advice to city planners and leaders: "Make big plans; aim high in hope and work, remembering that a noble, logical diagram once recorded will never die, but long after we are gone will be a living thing, asserting itself with ever-growing insistency. Remember that our sons and grandsons are going to do things that would stagger us. Let your watchword be order and your beacon beauty. Think big."

A male lifeguard walks along the sea wall checking the water level with some gadget. We chat about the erratic lake levels and how climate change is affecting them from year to year.[5]

---

5   Indeed, climate scientists are not sure how global changes will affect the Great Lakes. But there is mounting evidence that it has already altered Lake Michigan's mean temperatures, both at the surface and in its depths.

I feel for lifeguards. Having spent a few summers as a lifeguard myself, I know how monotonous and thankless the job can be. I've swum out with lifeguards in the panic of a search for a missing person. I've stood with them and the Chicago police in a circle on the shore as we all stared in silence at the body of a woman face down in the sand, the surf washing over her hair, a coat sleeve lifting and falling with each wave.

I begin to feel a slight pain in my left hip as the pitch of the boardwalk forces me to favor my left leg. The concrete offers no give either and there are miles more left before me. I haven't given much thought to how the conditions of my route and the repetitive movements of walking on concrete or asphalt might affect my joints or muscles. I continue on with a hitch toward the Loop.

Near Navy Pier, Chicago's Disneyland along the Lake, tourists crowd the narrowing Lakefront Trail as they meander back and forth from their nearby hotels. Like the tourists around me, I stop as I cross the river. Here is where Chicago began. If I look west toward the city rather than out into the harbor, I can see the architectural icons that stand on what was once a marshy wetland and piles of sandy silt where Chicago's first non-native resident, the aforementioned Jean Baptiste Point du Sable, and his Potawatomi wife erected their cabin and trading post. But while the river helped make this place a hub of trade and transit, its role changed when cholera outbreaks forced the city to consider the unthinkable—reversing it.

I look down at the perennially gray-green river that still seems confused as to which way it's supposed to go, out to the lake as its geography dictates or inland and backwards as engineers have designed. Locks of course keep it flowing into the Chicago Sanitary and Ship Canal and on into the Des Plaines River, backwards.

Walking makes me see how much the story of the city is a story of hydrology. The feats of engineering are on a scale that boggles the mind. The reversal of the Chicago River, the building of the Sanitary and Ship Canal, the tunnels under the lake to the intake cribs offshore, the city's sewar system and the maze of deep tunnels under the Loop. All go unnoticed as our eyes are drawn upward to the steel and stone towers erected by the master builders. But like the skyscrapers, the grand feats of engineering that manipulate the flow of water into and out of the city are here by the hand and muscled backs of Chicago's' anonymous workers. The

workers of the world did unite in Chicago, and they still do. Generation after generation, they have traveled by foot and horse-drawn wagon, by bus and train, by boat and plane, from farms not far away, from deep in the Delta of the Mississippi, from nearly every hamlet in Europe and Mexico, from each state and nation of Asia, Latin America, and Africa, from every island, every coastal city, cross-roads, and far-flung collection of huts and houses across the globe.

Humans, like everything that lives on this planet, are dependent on and part of the hydrological processes that have been at work since life emerged. We may think we have the technology and the brains to control water and atmosphere for our benefit and profit, but sometimes I think of that ferocious and prophetic voice that comes from the whirlwind, asking Job the obvious as he sinks to the ground in humility and awe: "Who put wisdom in depths of darkness and veiled understanding in secrecy? Who is wise enough to marshal the rainclouds and empty the cisterns of heaven, when the dusty soil sets hard as iron, and the clods of earth cling together?" (Job, 38:37)

Grant Park

From Lower Wacker's netherworld of steel and concrete, I follow the throngs of tourists under the Drive, back out into the sunlight and onto the trail again. Liberated by the water and the light, my eyes leap into the blue haze of the lake and afternoon sky where sailboats define the distant horizon to the east. Closer to shore, racing sailboats tack in tandem, red-and-blue-striped sails billowing in the wind. The Lakefront Trail curves inland toward the Loop, creating the northern boundary of Monroe Harbor. Here, the wealthy park their yachts and pleasure crafts next to the exclusive Chicago Yacht Club.

If I had a sport jacket folded inside this little pack of mine and a friend with a membership, I'd be able to take a seat at their upscale restaurant, the only one along this famous stretch of the lakefront. But I belong to the masses. I'm a pawn instead of a king. I have no yacht, no carriage, not even a horse. I'm but a commoner, a pedestrian—from the Latin "pedes," foot—a man on his feet, a man of the road.

Along with the lunchtime joggers, cyclists, suburban sightseers, and tourists, we pedestrians wait our turn to cross as three lanes of traffic blow by, first from the south, then from the north, and finally a flank of SUVs from the west, which speeds straight toward us before it makes a wide turn onto the northbound lane. That's nine lanes of cars all able to cut the legs out from under a living human being and toss them twenty or thirty feet into the air. Though Chicago's famous parkway has its admirers, no one who has spent any time here should be fooled by the lilies in the median or the landscaping along its route: DuSable Lake Shore Drive has always been an expressway designed to channel tens of thousands of motorists every hour of the day, particularly commuters to and from the Loop. It's a dangerous act to cross six lanes of traffic. It's not the most inviting entry into Grant Park, but then again, this grand old park has about as much concrete in it as green space. And when the light is green, I scurry across, worried for the tourists who are happily oblivious.

I've spent the last five hours on the lakefront free from that beast of steel and rubber that kills or maims people each day on Chicago's streets. Despite the city's efforts to extend bike paths, create greenways, and promote bike sharing, Chicago continues to experience increasing numbers of pedestrian injuries and deaths. Throughout the US, the numbers of pedestrian deaths have reached a forty-year high.[6] Though the Loop and the heavily populated lakefront neighborhoods are congested, these areas aren't necessarily where Chicagoans are in danger for their lives. In these parts of the city, there are crosswalks with lights that work. Here there are sidewalks fit to walk for miles. Here streets are not thoroughfares where motorists think they can speed. Here, "Chicago Works," as the Daley mayoral dynasty and famous machine often boasted, with their ubiquitous signage posted on every city project. But for those who live outside the lakefront neighborhoods of the North Side and the ever-expanding enclaves popping up around the city's Loop, these signs are few and far between.

This isn't a new story. The British journalist William T. Stead, who wrote *If Christ Came to Chicago* in 1894 after his visit to the city during the Chicago World's Fair, was appalled by the poverty he witnessed and shocked by the number of pedestrians hit and killed every day in Chicago by streetcars and trains. In *The Jungle*, Upton Sinclair famously details the awful working conditions in Chicago's meatpacking industry, but the book also is an exposé on the wretched neighborhoods, streets, and housing where these workers and their families lived. Both mention children hit by trains as they walked along railroad tracks gleaning for coal.

Chicago remains a city with two stories, two halves, one that shines and bustles and one that is hidden from view, behind the facade. So noted the French writer and philosopher Simone De Beauvoir after her first visit, when she toured the West Side bowery district with the bard of the city's underclass, Nelson Algren. Algren's social realism offered unapologetic portraits of the city's underbelly as well as the hustling ethic that defined both the high rollers and those working in the back alleys and bars, those running the brothels and the broken-down flophouses. He described a mid-century Chicago that crushed dreams and left people to the harsh fates once they were used up by the capitalist system.

---

6   According to the Insurance Institute for Highway Safety, there were 7,522 pedestrians and 1,084 bicyclists killed in 2022 and approximately 67,000 pedestrians and 46,195 bicyclists injured in motor vehicle crashes on public roadways in the United States. Pedestrians comprised about 18% of crash deaths, and bicyclists made up an additional 2%.

The real Chicago is one beyond the Loop of course, and if I really wanted to take a stroll through this metropolis, I'd walk down any of the north-south streets that cross the city from border to border, Ashland or Western, or any of a number of others that begin at the lake and head west, say Division or Devon, or I could take those old trails once made by the Potawatomi that follow the ridges of the old shoreline of Lake Chicago. By sticking to the Lakefront Trail, I'm not seeing the city that I know exists in that vast brick landscape to the west, populated by those I've taught and their families, enclaves centered around strip-mall grocery stores and churches, temples and mosques, restaurants and bars. While teaching I saw another Chicago—one of immigrants and of those who made it out of the housing projects and the struggling neighborhoods on the South and West Sides. These students wrote the real story of this city in fifty different dialects, detailing for me a map that I carry everywhere I go.

I hurry on, hoping to outrun the crowds and my growing doubt about whether I'll make it beyond the Loop. Though the sidewalks in Grant Park are wide enough for a truck, I find myself walking out into the street to pass photo-frenzied, selfie-taking tourists and waddling families four abreast toting oversized shopping bags.

Low blood sugar has set in, and I can feel the familiar droop in energy and mood. But physiology may not be the only reason my mood shifts as I head toward Michigan Avenue's stone wall, a showcase of American urban architecture. I have history here, as I do in half a dozen neighborhoods where I've lived and a dozen more where I've worked. The facade of buildings to the west—two planes meeting on Michigan Avenue—defines the horizontal and vertical geometry of Chicago. Like a line of occupying soldiers, shoulder to shoulder, these buildings, along with the Chicago River and the knot of multi-lane expressways circumscribing the commercial sector, collectively function as a fortress wall that separates the city center from the surrounding neighborhoods. The separation seems symbolic, perhaps, but if you know something of the city's history you know it's neither an accident nor simply due to geography. These sleek towers of steel and glass project the ever-growing disparities in wealth and power amassed by those on the top. Walking into it, the inspiration that I once felt in the first years I lived here has been replaced by a feeling of alienation. If this is the heart of the city, it beats not for me but rather only for a select few.

I feel a bit different about Grant Park, sentimentally referred to as "Chicago's front yard." It was first a railroad yard, in fact once the largest in the world. The massive railroad yard was built out of the mountains of debris left over after Chicago's devastating fire. Panoramic photographs give some idea of its enormity: forty or more tracks filled this space, fanning out across a field of earth black from coal dust and spillage. Wooden water towers rose out of the filthy, rat-infested landscape. The smoke and stench were legendary and often lethal for those who had to work there and for the throngs of transients who slept there. Hundreds died of respiratory diseases from the pollution billowing daily from the furnaces and from the coal-fired steam engines barreling through the city night and day.

The city center suffered from its success as the nodal point of America's railroads, with the smoke turning it unseemly and unhealthy. Burnham's Park therefore was built to revitalize and remake the city in order to present to the world, as his design for the World's Fair did, an American city that embodied the grandeur and sophistication of the capitals of Europe. Borrowing heavily from Georges-Eugene Haussmann's monumental modernization of the streets and parks of Paris, Daniel Burnham transformed the railroad yard into Grant Park using neoclassical landscape design and ornamentation: allees of elms outlining large lawns, promenades along rose gardens, and plazas with spherical fountains.

The word "Chicago" in my mind evokes the wind knocking me against strangers who hold me up as we walk along State Street, or encountering my neighbors while swimming far out into the lake and laughing as we discuss politics while treading water. A city is an organism that lives in our mind, created over a lifetime of encounters with its residents, human and nonhuman; its natural history, ancient and newly formed; and most certainly its history, alive in its built environment. The shell of a city may be spectacularly designed, as this one is, particularly in the Loop, with its flourishes of ornamentation and whimsy by the likes of Picasso and Sullivan, but its life is in the waves and winds that have shaped it and in the creatures and plants that inhabit it.

I could find something to eat in one of the outdoor eateries just to my right, in what has become the most heavily tourised twenty-five acres in Chicago—Millennium Park. But the lines will be long, and I can't stomach the park's built-in ads for its corporate donors, like BP's five-million-dollar "Pedestrian Bridge," designed by Frank Gehry

I cannot deny that the park has charmed the city and even brought in the suburbanites. I applaud the needed addition of twenty-five acres of green space, as well as Millennium Park's multi-use design, with Frank Gehry's modernist touches both in the bridge and in the highly prized sculpture of stainless steel atop the concert stage of the Pritzker Pavilion. And who can't be wowed by the abundance of public artwork: fountains, native gardens, and Anish Kapoor's ingeniously designed, bean-shaped "Cloud Gate" (the Bean), which brings the viewer into the center of a distorted mirror image of themselves with the swirling city and clouds above?

But coming in well over budget at a half a billion dollars, the park follows the city's long history of bowing to the whims of its wealthy barons and boosters, whose money has created here one more spectacle to dazzle tourists and bolster the city's image and their own while those who live outside the Loop and the lakefront neighborhoods must make do with sunless play-lots between apartment buildings, basketball courts under expressways, and asphalt parking lots behind local elementary schools. Would Burnham himself approve? Does the use of Millennium Park to host corporate parties violate the sacred decree that was at the heart of the grand Plan of Chicago, which famously states: "The Lakefront by right belongs to the people. Not a foot of its shores should be appropriated to the exclusion of the people . . . It shall forever remain always open and free."

I turn my back on the Millennium Park and cross Monroe Street to find some shade among the staid row of crab apple trees that outline the grounds of the old bandshell named for James Petrillo, the famous leader of the American Federation of Musicians who first brought free concerts to the city during the Depression and thus began a longstanding summer tradition in Grant Park.

I didn't set out on this walk to follow some historic path through my years in this city, but my mind seeks reference points to make sense of what I'm doing. Without even turning my head, I hear echoes of sound from the bandshell, the stage, the chairs, the weedy lawn, the over-flowing trash cans—chords from the city's juke box. How many musicians, how many songs can I hear, how many millions of clapping hands and dancing feet? How many bodies can I sense, wrapped around each other in the silvery city night?

At the corner of Columbus and Adams, I cut between shrubs on a path made over the years by students at the School of the Art Institute and traverse the manmade canyon of limestone blocks that funnels trains under the Art Institute and into the Illinois Central Station. Now that I'm on streets again and off the lakefront, more memories unmoor themselves as my eyes absorb this familiar path that I've walked to teach my classes at Columbia College and to other jobs I've had trying to make a living here. Along Michigan Avenue, I weave among musicians, weary tourists, panhandlers folded into their wheelchairs. Street vendors hawk t-shirts, knock-off White Sox hats, newspapers, and plastic bottles of water.

At an Italian eatery that serves pizza and dollops out healthy portions of pasta, I sink into a bone-hard metal chair at an outside table. For a moment, I simply sit and stare and let the marinara sauce tantalize my tired body. People eat their pizza and pick at their salads while I wipe my plate clean with my bread. Despite having just demolished a normal lunch, I look longingly at the counter and consider another helping of ravioli, but in the end I only allow myself a second iced coffee. I go ahead and eat the chocolate bar I was going to save for later, though.

With difficulty, I bend over, loosen my hiking shoes, and slip them off. My ankles have begun to swell, and my thighs throb, but though my toes are hot, I can move them without feeling any of the tell-tale tenderness that comes with blisters. I have no hip pain, no shoe problems. My body is holding up. The heat of the day has peaked. I've walked for some five hours, no small feat, maybe thirteen miles, but not even halfway to my destination outside of Gary. After filling up my cup with more water, I think of pulling out my maps to assess just what lies ahead of me. But I don't want to know how far I might have to go. I just want to keep walking.

Beyond the Loop my options and access to public transport will diminish. The farther I walk, the more difficult it'll be to make a retreat. There will always be taxis, though, or so I hope.

Across Michigan Avenue, I can see a line queuing for the 146 Express Bus. I could be home in half an hour: slump into a seat in the back, close my eyes, then glance out at the lake, and before I know it be back on Sheridan Road, my hand reaching for the cord to signal the driver to stop. I'd hobble up three flights of steps and close my door on Chicago like I've done thousands of nights before.

But I feel no compulsion to decide. Though my body senses the distance and anxiety of what lies ahead, I'm surprisingly content. Here I am surrounded by familiar images of this city I've lived in for thirty-odd years—the street names, the buildings, the hard angles, the colorless forms of concrete, the uniformity and drone of life in the Loop. I've traveled to this table on Michigan Avenue on foot, and because I have, I see the city with an altered eye. No longer is the city solely a set of well-worn impressions that I've constructed from habitual patterns of moving through it by train or bus, nor is it the city I've mapped in my mind for purposes of navigation by car or even bike. It is no longer a city that others have defined for me; walking is making it mine.

While I was walking all morning, my eyes were liberated from the ground, pulled out into the lake's expansive horizons and up into the sky, jumping far ahead to the skyline that disappeared and reappeared as I moved along the shore. Now, as I sit at a table on Michigan Avenue, the view is all foreground, all moving human bodies, arms swinging, hands holding bags and phones, legs scissoring in rhythms, and feet shod in shoes of all sizes, styles, and colors. Two flowing streams of torsos, one heading north, another heading south—intersecting paths passing before me within reach.

Leaning back in my chair, I follow the movement. As I watch the walkers, I start to focus only on the moving legs: the legs of the short and tall, the men and women, old and young, tourist and shopper, the worker, the suit-and-tie man. Then among a forest of legs I spot a chubby child stopping to reach for a prize on the sidewalk, only to be hoisted into the air by the arms of his mother. How little I know of my own legs. I watch those moving before me, making their way, each with a rhythm, a path, a destiny only their legs can follow.

Michigan Avenue to Soldier Field

Refueled with pasta and caffeine, I press on down Michigan Avenue, passing the iconic bronze sculptures of Plains Indian warriors, The Bowman and Spearman, astride their monumental stallions at the entrance of Grant Park. These sculptures were yet another piece of Burnham's Plan of Chicago. Burnham originally intended that only one would represent an Indian and the other would be a cowboy, supposedly to pay homage to both the Indigenous people and those who conquered them in the name of expansion. However, the victorious cowboy was ultimately omitted. These two prominent sculptures were commissioned by the Art Institute and carved by the Croatian artist Ivan Mestrovic, who'd never actually set foot in America or met an American Indian.

Though the artistry of these forms is majestic and aesthetically stunning, when I look at these idealized statues of naked warriors I can't help but remember the pained outrage on the face of an Ojibwe scholar and traditional medicine woman whom I'd invited to the Field Museum to give a lecture when I worked there back in the late 1980s. Living far to the north, on Beaver Island in the middle of Lake Michigan, she'd not been to Chicago since she was a younger woman and had forgotten the statues. But upon seeing them in such a prominent position in the park, she was so shocked that she stuck out her tongue at them as I drove her to the museum for the lecture.

Further on, crossing Michigan at Congress and walking along the gardens and benches, I pass another statue famous for more than just what

it represents—that of the Civil War general and Illinois politician John Logan. On this small mound before me, the statue of General Logan on his horse seems no more remarkable today than it did in the summer of 1968 when thousands of protestors swarmed around it as they held their ground against Chicago's police. Yet General Logan's statue among the sea of protesters became the image beamed around the world of America's war with itself that summer of 1968.

Now the men and women in blue buzz by on motorized Segways as they give directions to tourists and keep the bushes from becoming shelters for those with no housing. And there go two officers passing me, as they fly between two concrete planters full of leafy lime-green hostas, tiger lilies, and flowing pink petunias, thanks to the floral make-over of the Loop and Grant Park by the city's former mayor, Richard M. Daley (not to be confused with his father, Richard J. Daley, who was mayor from 1955 to 1976 and whose makeover of the city had more to do with the use of concrete).

Crossing once again over the canyon that holds the Illinois Central tracks, I head back toward the lake, pass under a canopy of tall elms, and make a dangerous dash across the six lanes of Columbus Drive. Dipping down into a twelve-acre plaza of grass that becomes softball fields in the summer, I stop before I reach the other side and look around at this empty field and the towers of the Loop in the west. It is here that I stood along with some two hundred fifty thousand other Chicagoans, and perhaps a billion more watching on screens from Hong Kong to Nairobi, as Barack Obama walked out onto a stage a couple hundred feet away as the 44th president of the United States.

Though this park holds grand public events, there are ghosts here, too, haunting these streets and parks in the Loop, memories that linger in and outside of this built landscape, secret memorials, private and public traumas, lost loves, dreams destroyed.

Back in the '90s there was a Chicago public health clinic a few blocks from the Loop on South Michigan Avenue. It was there where I sat one cold March afternoon in a waiting room full of young men and women, people like me, trying not to look terrified as we waited for what we didn't want to read on that slip of computer paper printed in dot-matrix: the results of our HIV tests. The public health clinic is now gone like much of the rugged urban environment of warehouses and furniture stores, parking garages and small-manufacturing shops that once defined the South Loop. I could have chosen to walk by it, but I've learned to stay away from places around the city that I associate with those lost years, when the future was a subject I learned to avoid in conversations. Sometimes I think a part of me is still there—a ghostly self, wandering those windy streets of South Michigan Avenue; a haunted, burdened figure, collecting the sorrows of each passing day, unable to forgive himself, unable to walk on.

Whether we create our own maps and overlay them onto the cities where we live or whether, in reverse, cities imprint their dramatic histories onto us, this phenomenon, known as psychogeography, becomes less abstract when one walks, particularly in cities and lands steeped in layers of human history.

In contrast to the flashy modernization represented by Millennium Park, I'm still partial to the staid and solemn south part of Grant Park, with its old fountains, flowering crab apple trees, stately columns of elms, and small statue of a humble Abraham Lincoln. Here you can sense the energy of the city flowing out to meet the incoming breezes off the lake and feel the temperature differentials as you walk east toward the water. To me, these trees bring the city's famed towers behind them into proper scale, tempering their dominating designs and rectangular forms. After a heavy snow or in early spring when their limbs awaken and lighten in color, their organic patterns contrast with the strong lines and architectural cubes of the skyscrapers. Unlike the city's prized sculptures—its Picassos, Calders, Dubuffets—these organic forms of public art grow with us as living witnesses to who we are. How easy it is over time to erase them from view as we become more and more absorbed with the distant and digitally derived.

Older trees are living forms of statuary, too. Here, they have withstood the harsh winters and rooted themselves in the city soil. Elsewhere, planted by the city or by its citizens, they miraculously have flourished, tunneling year by year under concrete, wrapping around pipes and wires, spreading their branches over alleys to seek the sun. They are everywhere if you have an eye for them. Those that I admire most arise on their own without plan or purpose, the trees that steal into parks or graveyards, running along railways and blooming behind brick buildings, widening crevices year by year in the concrete, breathing new life into the air for all the city's creatures.

A few hundred yards from Michigan Avenue, I stop and scan the impressive wall of stone buildings as well as the entire built environment all around me. I'm struck by how I could have passed all of this by so many times and not stopped to consider what is on display in a city like Chicago. Its skyline reflects not only the workers who've built the towering structures but also the forces of nature that come together in the never-ending building and creative production that go into making this metropolis function, many of which are easily overlooked: here among the iconic cultural centers and commercial towers is the limestone composed of compressed ancient life dug from nearby quarries and the hills of Southern Indiana. Here in the walls and floors are beams of wood grown from the soils of the forests of Wisconsin and Michigan. Here in the millions of windows that sheath the tallest skyscrapers is glass made from the silt and sand of long-ago oceans. Here in the frame of each building is steel forged from the iron ore of Minnesota with heat from the coal of Appalachia and Southern Illinois. All extracted, transported, processed, and eventually formed, soldered, hammered, crafted, and polished by the hands of workers.

I leave Grant Park by way of a wide, newly built walkway that descends under DuSable Lake Shore Drive and reconnects with the Lakefront Trail as it meanders between the Shedd Aquarium and that neoclassical monument to natural history and its benefactor, the merchandise magnate Marshall Field. Families mill about, dazed from a long day of dragging themselves through the halls and exhibits of the earth's origins, its creatures and plants, and its civilizations ancient and vibrantly alive.

As I scan the grand white marble steps of this mammoth mausoleum, I think of all those objects inside, encased in glass and stored away by the thousands, in boxes and wooden cabinets hidden in the bowels of the museum. I went to work in the museum's education department in the mid-1980s after abandoning graduate studies in theology at the University of Chicago. How fortunate I was, now that I think about it, to have had a job that required me to meet scientists and spend weekends walking through remnant prairies and down city streets, listening to the impassioned voices of botanists, cultural historians, and zoologists unveiling the unique story of Chicago's human and natural history.

I think of them there, those curators, in the rings of rooms unseen at the top of the museum, above the exhibit hall. And I recall how decades ago now they were signaling the alarm as their research and travels revealed to them shocking evidence of a decline in biodiversity due to climate change, development, deforestation, and pollution. It was at the Field Museum that ornithologists produced some of the key evidence for Rachel Carson's thesis in her ground-breaking environmental masterpiece *Silent Spring,* in which she showed that the unregulated use of the pesticide DDT was decimating birds as well as mammals and fish. By comparing the amount of DDT in species in the Field Museum's collections with birds that were dying in record numbers in the late 1950s, scientists here could clearly see that DDT became concentrated in certain species at the top of the food chain.

Often, I found that the best educators for the courses and fields trips I organized for the museum weren't necessarily the curators but instead the local naturalists and college professors. These experts knew every plant and species of trees, knew the geological story behind each river and moraine, knew the history of every building and neighborhood off the top of their head. They were keepers of the lore of forgotten habitats and storytellers of the city's textured social history. I am not surprised that my memory has called them forth as I make this trek along the shore to Indiana's dunes.

Reaching the end of the city's cultural monuments, the Lakefront Trail becomes more road than path as it functions to funnel fans from their cars, parked in the acres of asphalt that dominate the lakefront between these iconic cultural landmarks, to the city's gargantuan convention complex, McCormick Place. Although the city has spent a lot of money to make this stretch of the lakefront more accessible to the exploding numbers of young professionals who now reside in the gentrified neighborhoods of the south Loop, no matter how many trees you plant or tons of dirt you pile into faux hills around these dead spaces known as parking lots, they don't disappear. Despite Chicago's mass transit system, this is still a city built for the automobile. Hidden under Grant Park is one of the largest parking garages in the United States, with a capacity of something like eight thousand spots. Chicago is nothing like LA, where surface parking alone takes up a whopping 14 percent of the city's landscape and parking lots take up more space than housing! Still, at 3 percent, Chicago has a problem with the space devoted to housing and parking its cars—from parking garage zoning battles to actual fistfights among life-long neighbors over parking spaces cleared after the first winter storm.[7]

7 Daniel Herriges, "Parking Dominates Our Cities But Do We Really *See* It?," *Strong Towns*, November 27, 2019, https://www.strongtowns.org/journal/2019/11/27/parking-dominates-our-cities-but-do-we-really-see-it.

III

SOUTH SIDE

And I felt that this world, despite its massiveness, was somehow
dangerously fragile.

—RICHARD WRIGHT, BLACK BOY

McCormick Place to 31st Street Beach (Margaret Burroughs Beach)

Walking out from under the gloomy shadows of Chicago's hulking black steel and glass convention complex, McCormick Place, I find that apart from a few fishermen and an occasional cyclist for the first time in hours I have the trail pretty much to myself.

I can feel it like the chill in the air from a storm blowing off the Lake, the historic dividing line between Black south and white north in America's most segregated city. You might not readily sense this divide if you've never spent time in this city. But to a resident of more than three decades, who has lived on both sides of this divide and crossed from north to south hundreds of times, the difference is palpable, even passing through in a car going sixty miles per hour.

All over this city there are these lines, as there are all over America; some, thankfully, have been dismantled, while others remain literally built into the city's infrastructures—its streets, its expressways, its transportation systems, its schools and city services. Like other human inventions such as agriculture, industrialization, resource extraction, pollution, cities, roads, and war, race, too, has had its effects on geography.

Inland, across the Drive, mini skyscrapers of stacked condos rise in what was once a warehouse district of hulking brick buildings, for years a buffer zone between the North and South Sides. Gone are the infamous housing projects that once defined the skyline of the South Side and housed upwards of a quarter million residents. It still seems odd not to see them as I scan the skyline here to the west. Those sixteen-story concrete towers that lined the State Street corridor, conveniently clustered in groups and abutting the high fences and barrier of the ten-lane Dan Ryan Expressway, came down quietly in 2006.

On the lakefront, there is no visible sense that some line has been crossed from north to south. For years, the lakefront from McCormick Place south to Hyde Park was little more than a two-and-half-mile strip of weedy grass with stands of black oaks here and there. Until recently, if you ventured south beyond the small 12th Street beach on Northerly Island, there was one lonely beach at 31st and behind it some picnic tables and a playground. In recent years, however, the city has upgraded the beach facilities, rebuilt the retaining lake wall, and added another harbor.

As I pass through shadows of the eight-story McCormick Place and leave the Loop behind me, the lakefront landscape changes in function and style. No longer under the grandiose and stately influence of the city's great cultural and commercial structures, the park returns to its pastoral character and purpose: serving as a playground for the people who live nearest to it. But there is a new philosophy guiding the Park District these days. As planners and landscape architects finally give some attention to this section of the lakefront, I notice that where once there was grass a replica of the long-lost Illinois prairie now grows. Among the black oaks planted years ago sprout purple cone flower, joe pie weed, and other native grasses. In some places the plants have been burned to their roots to mimic the prairie fires that regularly enriched the soil and revived the root systems of these endemic species that once dominated the state. These changes are a welcome shift away from the common practices of commercial landscapers who are little interested in whether plants are native or not as long as they're cheap and hardy. And yet, looking at this laudable experiment, I wonder if these eco-friendly gardens of wildflowers and prairie grasses satisfy the ideals of planners rather than the needs of the people who use this portion of the lakefront. With its high grasses and clumps of woods, the area certainly isn't going to be used much for picnicking or playing.

With each step, I'm walking into both the future and the past. Walking has attuned me to the city's rhythms: its riffs and refrains, its shrill screams, its deadening silences, and in these vibrations, I feel a growing sense of longing. But for what? For some idealized and unexamined past that I'd rehearsed so often I believed it couldn't change? Perhaps because I've committed myself to this path between city and lake, the city's history is beginning to reveal itself, not as ideas and abstractions preserved in books or memorials, photographs or museums, but rather as stories alive in me and in every building, every tree, every human body I pass.

What is history if not a reckoning with the dead and their ghosts all around us? Not far away, just across Lake Shore Drive, it doesn't take much to conjure up the ghosts of the hundreds of dead Confederate prisoners, shuffling and starving and falling face-first in their own frozen shit at Camp Douglas just across the Drive, and then being tossed in mass graves until the land became too valuable and the city had them removed to a memorial outside of town.

And with them, you can see children sifting through the trash heaps around the stock yards. They're all still here, someplace, reaching out for you if you walk slowly enough to see their shadows. Helen Keller wrote, as she toured Chicago's tenements, of sensing the suffering all around her even though she couldn't see the faces and bodies, saying she could feel it in the hands of the children she touched.

Directly west of here, on the near South Side across the Chicago River, thousands of Irish workers settled in Bridgeport, purposely kept outside the city proper. Here they, along with Black men and anyone else who could hold an axe or shovel, dug the Illinois and Michigan Canal by hand—a canal that opened boat traffic to the Mississippi in the 1840s. They lived in what by all accounts was the city's first shantytown. Not only was there little affordable housing for workers or their families in the city, for the immigrant Irish there was little chance that they would be welcomed even if they had the money.

Two Black teenagers on either side of the trail approach as I pass and offer me a bike trail map for the South Side. "Do you like to bike?" a cheery girl asks, dutifully doing her summer job while her male counterpart stares down at a box at his feet full of maps. I thank them, and stuff it into my pack.

Three tiny Black children, all legs and arms sticking out of colorful bathing suits and caps, come running from the brand-new stone bathhouse, their mothers hustling behind warning them to stop. Thank God there weren't any cyclists cruising past. I glance out at the bathers in the water and those jumping about along the newly constructed beach. Almost all are children of color. A welcome sign, as so many children, particularly children of color in poorer areas of the city, have few opportunities to learn how to swim. According to the Center of Disease Control, Black children under the age of 15 are 3.6 times more likely to drown than white children.

Looking out at the children in the water splashing and screaming in the afternoon heat, I cannot keep an image out of my mind that haunts this part of the lakefront—that of a young Black teenager named Eugene Williams drowning not far from here on a hot day like this in the summer of 1919. Then there were no real beaches along this stretch of the lakefront then, nothing but rubble and debris and weeds. Nevertheless, those who lived directly west—the Irish of Bridgeport and the African Americans crammed into apartments and homes in Bronzeville—came in droves in summer to find some relief from the heat. That fateful July afternoon, as Black and Irish families gathered on the shore, no physical barrier separated the two South Side communities except for an unmarked dividing line that extended from shore out into the water. The so-called "color line" stretched even into Lake Michigan.

There are many versions of what happened, but Carl Sandburg provided the following account, written in a journalistic hand in the hope of helping city officials calm an anxious population:

> The so-called race riots in Chicago during the last week of July, 1919, started on a Sunday at a bathing beach. A colored boy swam across an imaginary segregation line. White boys threw rocks at him and knocked him off a raft. He was drowned. Colored people rushed to a policeman and asked for the arrest of the boys throwing stones. The policeman refused. As the dead body of the drowned boy was being handled, more rocks were thrown on both sides. The policeman held on to his refusal to make arrests. Fighting then began that spread to all the borders of the Black Belt.

Sandburg's report is a sociological analysis based on interviews and reporting that considers several factors that contributed to the racial tensions that still affect the city, among them housing, competition for work, the effects of war on Black soldiers coming home from World War I, and distrust in the city's police, political, and judicial systems. Sandburg, however, fails to note what historians now accept as another element that sparked the fury of Chicago's Black community on that day. Not only did the Irish policeman fail to arrest any whites for killing the Williams teen; instead, he made an arrest of a Black man caught throwing rocks at whites.

So, in truth, Eugene Williams didn't just drown—a mob of Irish youth stoned him to death while adults and a couple of Irish officers looked on and did little to stop them. The riots that erupted afterward reverberated across America, and the echoes have never really faded away. In the end, after several days and nights of fires, shootings, and battles in the streets and alleys, forty-eight people had been killed, hundreds wounded, and hundreds of Black families left without homes. (Chicago's fire and police departments, dominated by the Irish, let them burn, claiming the fires were out of control and too dangerous.) Without federal troops the city would have suffered far worse.

One disturbing footnote to Chicago's so-called race riot is the possible role that Richard J. Daley, the city's powerful mayor, might have played in the rampaging violence that spread throughout the city that week. Daley, then a teenager, was a member of the Hamburg Club, an Irish American organization that most historians agree was one of the key instigators of the violence and burning of Black homes. When asked about it years later, Daley denied any involvement in the violence, though only a few years after the infamous incident he became the president of the Hamburg Club. [1]

In my mind, the facts of this event—like all the facts of this city that have to do with race and power—sink to the sandy bottom of the lake when I imagine the scene of a boy trying to hang on to a splintery piece of lumber floating in the choppy blue waters that afternoon while rocks bombard him from the shore, striking his head, until he loses consciousness and drowns. What must it have felt like to be struck in the head by rocks while innocently swimming, not knowing what to do or why suddenly your life was in jeopardy? But on that July afternoon, the nightmare was only just beginning, and Eugene Williams was to be just one of the many victims of what became known as America's Red Summer, when racial violence exploded across the country, north, south, east, and west.

I've read that a small bronze plaque has been placed here in memory of Eugene Williams and the ugly riots of the summer of 1919. One might think the city would have created a monument to this young man to tell the truth about what happened here on the lakefront, next to the giant monument of commerce named for the city's iconic baron of manufacturing, Cyrus McCormick. But no. The plaque is thanks to a high school class in the suburb of Elmhurst, where students who learned about the riots raised money and asked the city for permission to put a small marker near the site where Williams drowned. The students chose to open their

---

1   William M. Tuttle, *Race Riot: Chicago in the Red Summer of 1919* (Champaign-Urbana: University of Illinois Press, 1996).

inscription with a quote from Martin Luther King Jr.: "A riot is the language of the unheard." And the memorial to the slain teenager ends with another of King's famous pleas to America and its racial legacy: "Darkness cannot drive out Darkness: only light can do this. Hate cannot drive out hate: only love can do this."

43rd Street to Promontory Point, Hyde Park

Hobbling on, I feel the effect of walking on a flat hard surface mounting from heel to hamstring to hip. Newly constructed basketball courts and a skateboard park appear, the sculpted surfaces of concrete with turns and jumps next to the familiar rectangle with its white circles and lines, neither in much use today. The Drive, too, looks spiffed up, the medians flush with flowers and shrubbery. From a car, entering from the south, the city looks grand with its castle-like pillars of steel and glass. Across the Drive, through brambles and thicket that in places camouflage the Illinois Central tracks, are the neighborhoods of Rosemont and Kenwood, just to the west. Now, finally, the city has begun to construct monumental walkways to link these neighborhoods, long disconnected, to this strip of lakefront.

Since setting out, my mind has floated from present to past, conjuring up events and people's faces, conversations, emotional flourishes, odd flashbacks—and with them other travels and walks, too, have followed along. My walking self seems to be a separate self with a backstory of its own, existing, seeing, and feeling, but solemn, only observing, until its language is heard.

How much of our story and its meaning lives not in our memory but in the landscapes that shaped it, gave it context, and infused it with light and sound, amplifying it so that we could feel and hear its echo?

The trail rises to meet a caged walkway over DuSable Lake Shore Drive at 43rd Street. From there Hyde Park and its lonely peninsula, Promontory Point, come into view, and with them the bittersweet memories of my three years here as a graduate student after my stint in the Peace Corps.

After over fourteen miles on the Lakefront Trail, I've reached part of it that looks almost the same as it did in the mid 1980s when I lived in Hyde Park. To my tender and tired feet, the grass looks soothing. So, stepping off the asphalt, I take off my shoes, hoping the softness of the grass might ease the remaining few hundred feet to Promontory Point, where I've planned to stop and rest.

The park at "The Point," as Hyde Parkers affectionately call it, looks unchanged from my student days: the "steps" of stone are as rough and weedy, students lie languidly in the grass, Hyde Parkers linger and stroll. Built in the 1930s with assistance from FDR's Works Progress Administration, Promontory Point, like the rest of the lakefront, is landfill. This twelve-acre park that juts out into the water off 53rd Street reflects Daniel Burnham's grand designs for the Lakefront on the South Side, where he'd envisioned islands just offshore, inland lagoons, boathouses, public beaches, lavish gardens, and groves of trees.

Though its original landscaping is gone, Promontory Point reveals the influences of the pioneering landscape architect Jens Jensen on the city's parks, with its use of native species of trees, local stone, and designs based on nearby natural environments. The Danish American was an early advocate for the expansion of public parks in Chicago, helping to establish the Forest Preserves of Cook County. As a founding member of the Prairie Club of Chicago, he was also one of the early proponents of preserving the

Indiana Dunes for both environmental and recreational reasons, recognizing the public health benefits of outdoor exercise and nature for workers and their families living in the overcrowded neighborhoods in and around Chicago.

As in Rogers Park, residents of Hyde Park are defiantly protective and assertive when it comes to the city's power, and they rejected the concrete slabs and uniform designs imposed on the lakeshore elsewhere, demanding that the WPA's limestone rocks be reset where they'd eroded from waves and winter weather. For now, they've been left as is, broken and worn from years of heavy and joyous use.

But as I walk in the thick grass toward the rocks, the memory that comes to me is, surprisingly, not of those days in the early 1980s but rather of my first glimpse of Lake Michigan and of this city on a trip with my family in the mid-sixties. For a boy who'd seen little more than soybean fields and stands of corn, the lake's sudden appearance after a day of driving through rural and industrial Indiana made a deep impression. Not only was the sight of such a vast span of water mesmerizing, but the very width and depth of the landscape was novel to me. Explosions of water shot up into the air as they slammed into the rocks, timed, it seemed, by some mechanical force. I followed each wave with my eyes as it rolled and crashed. I begged my parents to take me to see the lake up close. Who wanted to see displays of the "Kitchen of Tomorrow," or the many uses of soybeans, or those nightmarish fetuses floating in jars of formaldehyde at the Museum of Science and Industry? I wanted to run to the shore and stare out at that endless wave-making monster that went on and on until it became the sky.

I climb onto the rocks along this well-used spit of land, where students bask in the sun reading their paperback Penguin classics. Here and there, trees of heaven fan out of crevices where broken bottles and trash have been lazily stashed. Four boys on bikes bounce across the grass to the rocks, throw down their wheels, and leap down the stone steps to the water. They fling off their shoes and shirts, and without hesitation navigate the uneven rocks and jump in. They look more like large birds as their bodies hop and fly from one action to the next.

Carefully, I follow them down from the stone steps, feeling each joint and muscle as I descend the dangerous terraces of stone, bracing myself with my hands and pushing away broken glass with my feet as I go. Finally,

I sit down on the wet ledge of limestone and slowly lower myself into the water. Though the revetment wall has crumbled, and its iron pilings stick up out of the water, the lakebed is shallow, sandy, and quite clear and clean. Nothing could be more medicinal to my feet and sore muscles than sinking into the cool water and soft sand. For a few moments, I stand, letting my toes spread, and absorb the pleasure until I put my hands together over my head like a boy and dive into the smooth water. I take a few breast strokes, then turn on my back and float. Numb with fatigue, I'm content to look at the cloudless sky and listen to the excited voices playing and splashing nearby.

On the rocks, I let the late afternoon sun dry my body while I massage my feet, noting the swelling and flatness, but thankfully no blisters. After hours of looking far off into the expanse of the lake and up into the towers of the city's skyline, I now focus on what I hold in my hand inches away—the soles of my feet. I take my time examining my toes, realizing how rarely I look this carefully. The shape and scars of my feet tell stories of the past: the enlarged spaces between my toes from wearing sandals for two years in Senegal; crescent-moon-like scars from cuts and injuries in high school sports; the violet capillaries in the ankles I've inherited; the hardened skin from a long life of holding up this aging body. How strangely formed they are. How surprisingly individual. How remarkable this family of five that works together, sharing the burden of weight while pushing and guiding the body wherever it goes. A quarter of my body's bones are hidden here in my feet. How well-designed they are to hold weight and move the body with such dexterity over different types of terrain, feeling their way as they translate and navigate the living earth. There below, operating seemingly alone, at the extreme edges of the brain, how easily they are taken for granted.

Sometimes I wonder if the fatigue we feel as we age comes not from overworked muscles and weary bones but rather from years of habitually detaching the mind from what truly forms and gives the body its health, the living earth itself.

Putting on my socks, smoothing out the wrinkles on the bottoms of my feet, I can hear the voice of my father, the high school coach, showing me how to prevent blisters. I pull on my hiking shoes, careful to tighten the laces as snugly as I can, my hands working as they were taught.

It's closing in on five o'clock. The heat has barely diminished. The Drive is filling with traffic. The after-work crowd and students begin to file out of the concrete tunnel under DuSable Lake Shore Drive onto the trail and away from their day indoors. I notice more bikers and joggers, more children with parents, even a few solitary walkers like me. It would be pleasant to lie here in the grass or sit on a bench and read as the afternoon lazily drifts into evening, a most excellent time to be out at "The Point" as I recall.

I walk on to the other side of the peninsula and head back to the Lakefront Trail, scanning the tiered steps and looking out into the small bay created by another concrete jetty a couple thousand yards further south. I can see a few swimmers making their way from buoy to buoy on their way to the jetty at 59th street.

Here, many years ago, I followed other students and became a lake swimmer, inspired by the tribe, old and young, who have come to the lake (some all year long) to take their exercise in these waters off Hyde Park. I'll never forget the first time I came upon a foursome in late October, bobbing about in the surf far offshore. I watched dumbfounded, following them as best I could, wondering if, as they seemed no match for the large waves, I should call for help or try to save them myself. Only to discover, as they finally made their way back to shore, that they'd been swimming here for years. To my astonishment, all had to be well over seventy, maybe older. As they toweled off, their pink flesh glowed in the breeze, big-armed and silver-haired women and round-bellied and hirsute men.

"Isn't it cold?" I managed, standing above them on the rocks.

"Cold? Naaah, not cold. Good for you!," a man bellowed back in a distinctly Eastern European accent, pulling himself up to his full height, charcoal chest hair as long as his fingers springing out of his happy chest.

I was on one of my many walks that day, agitated and unable to study, which was so often the case when I was a student at the University of Chicago. I often came to the lakefront when the weather was bad or at night. The sound of the waves slamming against the rocks and the feel of the winds whipping in from the northwest comforted me. But it was the lake itself I needed most during that difficult time. When there was nowhere else to turn and no one left to trust, I learned that here in this cold concrete city, the lake was always there. Ancient and impartial, the lake is a witness to the struggles of all those who have come here for a better life. It does not offer human warmth as we know it, no pity whatsoever. It offers no opinion, no theological solace, no moral authority, no romantic succor. The lake speaks only in geological terms, in elemental metaphors, and most of us have little training in reading these oracular signs. Often, we misunderstand its meaning, mistaking the feeling of our despair for something in its distant and discolored depths. Ironically, in our moments of spiritual torment and inexplicable suffering, we recognize that the lake is no mirror, no resource, no force to be tamed. Instead, like all the great wonders of the earth, the lake reminds us of our elemental origins and ephemeral nature. If, even for a moment, you can feel this obvious truth and let it soothe your seething anger or sadness, you can light another cigarette, turn back towards the city, and walk home.

57th Street Beach to Jackson Park

From "The Point," the Lakefront Trail becomes all that separates 57th Street Beach from DuSable Lake Shore Drive, that, and a knee-high concrete wall. The winds shift as the shoreline now turns southeast toward

Gary on Indiana's coast. Along with the shift in the wind, my mood has changed as well. The swim has reinvigorated my muscles and confidence.

DuSable Lake Shore Drive effectively ends in Hyde Park, continuing on into South Shore Drive, splitting off into the university campus and on around the museum where it feeds into Stony Island Boulevard.

The intensity of the heat has mellowed, and the glare of the sun no longer washes away the distinctions of color. The golden hours of late afternoon have arrived. The lake, too, has now changed, darkening in color and undulating more freely as it laps up against rocks and the revetment wall.

Hustling along, trying to think myself forward as I have all day, I imagine where I'll be in an hour. Surely, I can make it to the state line by six, five-thirty if I push, and on to my hotel near Gary before dark?

My lake swim has energized me, but my eagerness to keep moving has something to do with where I am and where I'm headed. I'm about to exit this long-distance Lakefront Trail, enter the neighborhoods of the far South Side, and walk through stretches where the most vulnerable are subject to random violence simply because they're in the wrong place at the wrong time. These days in Chicago, and in America, it seems random violence can strike anywhere and anyone. The chances, however, are much higher in the poorest areas of the city, where Chicagoans of color are both perpetrators and victims of seemingly senseless crime. Here, as elsewhere in Chicago, there are pockets where the abnormal has become normal, and a child getting ready for bed or playing in the backyard can be shot with a body-shattering bullet.

No longer on landfill nor cut off from the city by the Drive, memories and the emotions they evoke pull me inland toward the neighborhood and campus where I once lived. I'm not sure if it's because I've been walking now for over eight hours or because of where I am walking, through a landscape etched into my mind, but perception seems to be playing tricks on me. Looking at the landscape of Hyde Park, I can see myself walking along the lake or heading back to my apartment or to the library down these familiar streets, passing the same trees, the same buildings, as if the decades have never passed.

In the late summer of 1983, I entered Divinity School here at the University of Chicago almost directly after returning from serving in the Peace Corps. High on the potent drug of pride at being invited to study in such a storied school, I arrived unprepared to either study or live in a segregated island surrounded by America's second largest Black community.

Consequently, almost from the beginning of my studies here, I felt conflicted as I tried to reconcile the stark divides I witnessed in the world outside of this rarified campus, not to mention the turmoil I felt within after leaving Senegal, my work, and friends with whom I'd become so close, particularly a fellow woman volunteer I'd fallen in love with. I was in mourning and confused as to why I'd left her and my work in West Africa to sit in seminars on moral philosophy and the theology of liberation. Living among subsistence farmers whose futures were being held hostage by international bankers and global markets, I had found my politics and views on America's role in the world upended. In Senegal, too, I witnessed the real effects, even then in the early 1980s, of environmental injustice as farmers were left with few options to eke a living for themselves and their families, planting crops that depleted their soils and grazing animals in landscapes denuded of grasses. I saw how vulnerable and dependent people had become as markets from abroad controlled what they could buy and what they could sell and at what cost.

On the South Side and beyond into Indiana I saw another version of what was happening globally. Here, where deindustrialization and Reagan's draconian policies were dismantling once vibrant communities, my eyes were opened once again to whose lives were being sacrificed. Thanks in part to courses and professors I had, I learned to equate the economic and racial injustice so evident in the landscape all around the university and into Indiana with the environmental degradation I could see all along the shores of Lake Michigan.[2]

And yet, the more I learned the more frustrated I became, not only with the role of the university in perpetuating the racial inequities in and around Hyde Park but also with myself for doing little more than sitting around on bar stools with my fellow classmates railing at what we saw with our newfound knowledge and slogans. Before I left my studies, I did join a community-based group of seminarians and clergy, and as part of

---

2   I had several influential professors while attending Divinity School and the Unitarian seminary Meadville Lombard. Among them were the theological scholars Martin Marty and Langdon Gilkey; the environmental historian and author of *Sacred Sands: The Struggle for Community in the Indiana Dunes*, J. Ronald Engel; and the professor of theology and religious studies at Catholic Theological Union, Claude Marie Barbour.

our work, I assisted immigrants—Hmong and Eritreans—who'd newly arrived in the city. But it was a drop in the bucket compared to the needs that seemed to multiply the more time you spent outside the university's ivy walls.

Now, as I walk on out of Hyde Park into the Woodlawn neighborhood, I can just barely see the bell tower of Rockefeller Chapel over the trees, another monument to add to all the others I'd seen since stepping out onto Sheridan Road. John D. Rockefeller provided funds to establish the university's endowment while Marshall Field provided the land; thus in a matter of years the city's wealthy were able to create a university that rivaled in stature the elite Ivy League schools of the East. If I climbed up into the bell tower, I could get a good view of where I was headed. I'd be able to see the refinery that Rockefeller's money built along the Lake well over a century ago. I'd be able to see much of the South Side and into the communities of Indiana, neighborhoods that have struggled since well before I came to Chicago. And though the housing projects have been razed, I would see pretty much what I saw as student here decades ago, traveling from North to South on a bus to Hyde Park—no doubt much the same, too, as what the city's truth-telling poets have borne witness to over the past century and more. Those clear-eyed social critics, Upton Sinclair and Ida B. Wells. Those chroniclers of the lives of the working poor such as Jane Addams or Richard Wright, or those who spoke of the pain of the neglected and sacrificed like Nelson Algren or Gwendolyn Brooks.

As I walk along the lakeshore, I feel an upsurge of energy from the people around me, basketball players in the parking lot playing five-on-five, cyclists racing along, athletic women and men out for their runs, meandering couples of every age and skin color.

Across the Drive is Fredrick Law Olmsted's arboretum, behind the Museum of Science and Industry. Here, where ladies and gentlemen once strolled along during Chicago's great Columbia Exhibition, scholars and students now come to muse and meditate, as did those before them, like the philosophers John Dewey and Paul Tillich or champions of the people Clarence Darrow and Senator Paul Douglass. It's also home in the early mornings to bird enthusiasts and a gathering place in the afternoons and evenings for queer Black men from the neighboring community.

Looking at Olmstead's trees and lagoons, I imagine the layers of life and history this land has witnessed as the former marshes and sand dunes were transformed by workers and gardeners into the grand White City of Burnham's World's Fair. Millions came to Chicago's South Side to marvel at the new age at hand, here in a city that had grown as big as Paris in a matter of decades. The Fair was, in a sense, a celebration of Chicago's symbolic rise not only out of the prairie but out of the ashes of the Great Fire two decades before. Jackson Park and the grounds of the Museum of Science and Industry are remnants of the White City, the artificial world erected to introduce Chicago as a city of the future, powered by the bountiful riches of the Midwest's landscape, capitalism, and technological innovation. I don't think those leaders of Chicago would have ever imagined a future in which this very land would house the presidential library of the nation's forty-fourth president, a mixed-race man from Chicago whose mother was a white anthropologist and father an economist from Kenya. It's unfortunate, to say the least, that to build the twelve-story Obama Library nearly six hundred of Olmstead's grand trees had to be cut down. This sparked outrage by many citizens that developers couldn't save more of the trees in their design.

Past 62nd Street Beach, a few families and children play in the late afternoon sun. I can see a group of young men playing ball at a court in a corner of a parking lot for the beachgoers. Full court, shirts versus skins, basketball is still the sport of Black Chicago, and you can find courts everywhere—in alleys, schoolyards, church parking lots, under the expressway, behind union halls, by loading docks and fire stations, and at the local Y. In my teens I, too, lived on a basketball court. Too slow and too short, I never made it past my high school team, but I played a lot in my adult life. Until I benched myself, thinking I might infect someone, succumbing to the social panic and fear of HIV/AIDS. But before that, I was that pain-in-the-neck white guy at the Y who blocked out and called fouls. A coach's son and purist from Indiana, what can you expect? I loved playing at the Y, where bus drivers could pass the ball to teenagers from the Cabrini Green housing projects, former college players, and other old dudes like me, as well as to young Black women who could humble any man who dared to disrespect their game.

Ahead lies Jackson Park's Harbor, and as I pass the old boat house, I come upon another prime fishing spot. Every twenty yards or so, an older Black man or woman sits hunched in a lawn chair, arms on knees, leaning toward the water, brimmed hat hiding their face, tackle boxes and

Styrofoam coolers close at hand. Practiced in the patient art of the rod and reel, their bodies are as much a part of the landscape here as the expensive boats and stone bridges and walkways through Olmsted's arboretum. They remind me of my grandfather, sitting on the edge of his pier on the small lake in northern Indiana where, after decades of factory work, he built a small cottage and retired in the 1960s.

Like many men I knew in my boyhood growing up in north central Indiana, my father and grandfather fished wherever and whenever they could—at night and early morning, from bridges and boats, in ponds and lakes, and in gravel pits and polluted rivers. As with these couples here along the harbor, I see and feel the same sense of restfulness I remember seeing in my father and grandfather, who cherished their time away from the world of work and words. Sitting in silence by the water or drifting about in a boat was a worthwhile pursuit, and I learned that even if I didn't much care for the snagging of bluegill with old hooks and dead bait, the purpose was to be out-of-doors and away from the hubbub, doing something with one's hands and eyes that wasn't work.

How serene they look, these men and women here, staring at their poles and those pencil-thin, red-tipped bobbers. Mesmerized by the water and the stillness before them. They make me long for the same serenity.

As I watched my parents age, lose memory and mobility, then curl into their final poses, I became more aware of what recreation means for older adults and how their health declines without it. In the parks and on the streets, I now notice those bound to wheelchairs, after seeing the world from walking behind my mother's wheelchair. All along the lakefront now, not just today but every day, I see them: mostly elderly women and their caregivers, sitting together on benches or rolling along, with a caregiver pushing them in a wheelchair. The caregivers are almost all women of color, immigrants from Africa, from the Caribbean, from Mexico, from the Philippines, and Black women from these neighborhoods around me.

Seeing these urban anglers makes me think of the many thousands trapped in lonely rooms, in wheelchairs, in bodies that can't move without pain. I think of the many people fearful of the streets, people who have no bicycles, people who live too far away from the lakefront or nearby parks.

In the summer of 1995, Chicago suffered one of the worst public health disasters in American history, when over seven hundred people succumbed to heat-related deaths. After two weeks of record-breaking heat, culminating in a string of 100-degree days, the city's poorest neighborhoods and most vulnerable citizens filled the city morgue to capacity as body after body was discovered. By far the largest number were older African Americans, mostly men living alone in the city's poorest neighborhoods on the South and West Sides. The city government was unprepared for what happened, revealing the general disparity in its services to poorer neighborhoods as well as denial about the environmental and social deterioration of many of the city's poorest Black neighborhoods.

Near the end of the lakefront stands the old South Shore Country Club, now the South Shore Cultural Center. Walled off with its fence and brick gate, it reminds me of Chicago's past, when this lakefront refuge was off limits to Catholics, Jews, and people of color. Its Mediterranean red-tiled roof and gables, carriage stables, nine-hole golf course, beach, ballrooms, and nature preserve are now open for all to use and enjoy.

Rounding the last hundred yards of the Lakefront Trail, I turn onto a sidewalk and head south along South Shore Boulevard, the lake now hidden from view.

South Shore Cultural Center to South Chicago

Back on a sidewalk after some nineteen miles, I re-enter residential Chicago by way of South Shore Boulevard, which will take me the last four or so miles through the neighborhoods of South Shore, South Chicago, and East Side until I reach the Illinois-Indiana state line. It's a little after five, and I've just passed one more chance to bag it by getting on the No. 6 Jeffery Express bus back to the Loop. But this is the walk I envisioned, one that sews the Lakefront Trail together with the communities and industrial landscape to the south and east. I can't quit now.

Though South Shore once was solidly middle class, full of charming brick high-rises with stunning views of the lake and the city skyline to the north, over the years parts of this neighborhood away from the lake have suffered, along with the rest of the South Side, from precipitous losses in America's manufacturing sector and pernicious racist practices in lending and housing. Right by the lake, however, are some of the only private residences along Chicago's entire lakefront. On a short block just east of South Shore Drive, rip-rap (boulders and loose stone) protects this block of homes, guarding them from the lake's tumultuous winter waves. I've always admired this corner of the city and this hidden lakefront neighborhood. There is a unique stylishness about these prairie-style homes with their juniper topiary, rich scarlet roses, and manicured yards and gardens.

Walking along South Shore in the shadow of these vintage high-rises confirms a feeling I've had before about this South Side neighborhood along the lake. As in Rogers Park, here there is a sense that you are no longer in Chicago. Wandering down South Shore Boulevard, I glance back north, and perhaps it's because I've been walking, but the skyline and even the lake look unfamiliar. The choppy opaque waves give it an ominous quality. But then, when I notice a young Black couple sitting romantically on a brick wall, looking out at the water and city skyline, the lake immediately seems to soften.

Though buses heave and hiss as they stop to let people off at every other corner, I don't see many people on the street until a young Black woman comes out of one of the high-rises and walks toward me. As she gets closer, I suddenly feel self-conscious. But why? Because I'm a white man and a stranger on her street? Like her, I'm just walking on a sidewalk on a summer afternoon, in a city where we both live. As she passes, our eyes meet, we nod and verbalize a faint "hello." At once my self-con-sciousness and anxiety drain away. How easily other people can alter our emotional states, I think, as she goes on down the street. How important these old-fashioned social graces are, not only to our individual health but also to that of our neighborhoods. Jane Jacobs, the influential urban-ist and author of *The Death and Life of the American City*, saw that our small, ordinary encounters on the sidewalk are, in the end, the interac-tions that create dynamic communities. The essence of a city's "order" and its "freedom" is for Jacobs the "intricacy of sidewalk use, bringing with it a constant succession of eyes."

Only once since I began my walk has anyone recognized me, and she was a former student buzzing by on her bike. As public and communal as the lakefront path is, nobody has greeted me and few have returned eye contact—not that I was trying to look people in the eyes myself all the time, though a few times, confronting another lone pedestrian, I did try. But here on a neighborhood street it's different. Or is it something else, something about differences in cultural attitudes toward greeting strangers on streets? In any case, the decorum and ritual of human greeting deserves more credit than we give it as we rush about, clutching our devices, feign-ing busyness, our eyes easily averted away from who is before us.

In cities, our pathways are not trails but sidewalks, communal pas-sageways that do much more than simply get us from point A to point B. A nod, a smile, a wave from across the street signals both "you belong" and "I belong." As someone who lives alone, on a day when I don't teach a greeting can be my sole human interaction for that day. I walk along the beaches hoping for interactions. I frequent my cafes, eager to say hello to the owners and staff. The Ethiopian café in my neighborhood is a second home for me. The Latino man who owns the grocery where I go three times a week always makes a point to greet me. It's the quality of interac-tions that are so crucial for us, the eye contact, the smile, the small talk, the pat on the back. The physical interaction is crucial not only for one's mental health but for the health of a city. Greetings matter.

As I head south, the apartment complexes become smaller and less ornate, two- or three-story affairs with courtyards. Homes, too, are now more uniform, and more and more of them reveal the effects of the housing crisis of 2008 as well as the long-term decline of the whole area since the shuttering of US Steel's South Chicago plant in the eighties. But

I shouldn't be surprised, as these neighborhoods were precisely the ones targeted by the shady schemes and predatory loans that brought on the whole housing collapse. Worse, local institutions like the South Shore Bank, a model for how banks could work to foster economic and community development, were forced to close. Though there are many intersecting factors that have contributed to the hollowing out of vast sections of the city's South and West Sides, the residual effect of discriminatory practices like redlining has been devastating. Failure to maintain schools, roads, sanitation, and other basic community services is also a form of redlining, not to mention the absence of health clinics, parks, grocery stores, and adequate public safety.

Perhaps it's me and my eye for gardens and landscaping, but just as one or two empty houses can bring this sense of gloom, another house next door can brighten the whole street. The roses around the wrought-iron gate and the orange snapdragons leaning against the side of the house eclipse in one glance the coldness of the empty house next door.

Down the block, a young Black man with a dolly rolls a used refrigerator to the curb and struggles to pull it up onto the sidewalk. In stride, I call out, "Need some help?" But as I get there, jogging the few yards to the double-parked pick-up truck, another young man from a nearby porch hops down the steps and arrives first. He glances quickly at me to see just who I am, then drops his eyes to the ground and mumbles his appreciation, "We got it okay, thanks."

Walking on, I wonder if I've violated some code in offering my help in such a public way, as a stranger to the neighborhood. Or has walking all day distorted my social response? I'm not sure. In a car, we don't feel obliged to stop, not in a city—not even if we see an accident. But on the sidewalk, in the sphere of the commons, aren't we "our brother's keeper"?

I'm anything but invisible, or so I think. At the next corner I notice that there are four teenage boys. I stiffen, pick up my pace, and try my best to appear nonplussed. Then from across the street, here comes another teen riding his bike. Even though it's a major thoroughfare, I know anything can happen on any given street in Chicago to anybody walking alone or especially to any group of Black teenage males. But the teenagers barely notice me, moving to let me pass.

From out of nowhere a cyclist on a road bike speeds by, reminding me that I'm walking along one of the city's many new biking routes through the South Side. This one extends the Lakefront Trail to Calumet Park a couple of miles further south and then continues east into Indiana.[3] Though parts of it can be used by pedestrians, much of it is on streets and roads. The urban biking revolution has firmly taken hold in Chicago and transformed this city, as it has elsewhere. The rails to trails program, the wildly popular rental bikes, and other initiatives have transformed the streets as more and more people take to their bikes.

The benefits of biking for physical and environmental health are obvious. But this revolution in transportation also changes our relationship with the city, making us more conscious of how it is built and how it affects our quality of life. Just as with walking, on a bike you see the city differently and feel its dead zones, places obviously built with nothing in mind except moving people and goods back and forth in the most efficient way, as if a city were nothing but a giant factory. My spirits are lifted when I see someone on a bike traversing beyond the Lakefront Trail and I am inspired by their self-sufficiency and working body. Though for every twenty-five-year-old commuting on a single speed rebuilt bike or those buzzing by on their $3000 dollar Cannondales or e-bikes, I think of those laboring on cheap bikes on their way to work early in the morning or coming home late at night in unlit parts of the city or suburbia where there is often no thought for bike commuters as everyone is expected to travel by car.

Cyclists are creating new pathways through these isolated urban and industrial corridors. I'm glad to see this cyclist buzz by, glad to see his athletic body churning his thin wheels, glad that he, in a way, normalizes what I'm doing. And yet as he speeds by, standing up in his stirrups, his thick thighs pumping with effort to increase his speed, he makes me aware that cyclists are less vulnerable and less at the mercy of the vicissitudes of a pathway. On foot, by contrast, one feels the ground, the dirt, the roots and stones, the concrete. One must commit to being there on the street and confront what's there rather than just moving through it. I use a bike in the city like many people do—to shop, to socialize, to commute, as a means of transport—but I rarely take it on adventures or out for pleasure.

---

3   The Marquette Greenway extends the Lakefront Trail 58 miles from the far South Side of Chicago, through Indiana, to the southeastern Michigan city of New Buffalo. With support from state, local and federal funds, this non-motorized trail is still under construction in many sections but is scheduled to be completed in 2026.

Perhaps this walk will change that. There are lots of converted railway paths and urban pathways being built, and though they are theoretically for pedestrians, by and large they're made and used for cyclists.

Block by block, zigzagging along the lake, South Shore Boulevard takes me from the elegance of the South Shore to South Chicago, the beginnings of the industrial crescent, and the cities and neighborhoods that I'll be walking through for most of the next thirty-five miles along this coast.

South Shore Boulevard heads around Rainbow Beach and Park, a sixty-acre park that has served both South Shore and South Chicago neighborhoods for one hundred years, though until the late sixties it was a whites-only beach. To the south lies the rather controversial two-mile stretch of empty land that was once home to US Steel's South Works—until it closed and the land reverted to a lakefront brownfield.

Inland again, I press ahead along a row of two-story wooden homes with walk-up porches, typical of this working-class neighborhood that abuts the industrialized depot and port of Chicago along the Calumet River a mile or so ahead. On the corner of 83rd and South Shore is Saint Michael's Catholic Church, with a tidy brick school attached, built by Polish immigrants who worked in the mills and dominated this neighborhood. Across the street is one of the city's classic neighborhood parks, a shady block square with an empty baseball diamond and a few other amenities. A man sits on a chair on his porch; a few doors down, there's a whole crowd of kids and two or three young women. A baseball diamond, an old Catholic church, a shady park—what could be more quintessentially Chicago? Then, suddenly, a car full of young men streaks by, shouts echoing from the car and back from the young women on the porch. The crescendo of energy is like a clap of thunder, sending a shiver of fear through me. But it's just a burst of youthful excitement, young men showing off for young women on a late afternoon.

Around the next zag on South Shore Boulevard, I am back near the brownfields by the lake. Here's a tire fix-it shop, painted bright red. But next to it, where there was once a grocery and some other businesses, windows and doors have long been boarded over. Just past them there is a three-flat apartment and then two homes covered in old tar shingles like those houses in the neighborhood where I grew up.

Two little girls riding tricycles peddle up and over a buckled sidewalk. Behind the houses an urban woodland has grown in one of the many abandoned railroad beds that once crisscrossed through this neighbor-hood. And hidden here and there in the tall stands of weeds and thick growth of honeysuckle and Chinese elm, I can see broken cars that years ago had become fixtures in these strips of urban edgelands.

Further on I pass a fire-engine-red brick Baptist church with freshly cut grass surrounding its concrete foundation, then a fenced lot next to it that now is thick with trees and littered with trash. Across the street are more collapsing three-flat apartments, some abandoned, some not, the yards behind them overgrown with thicket as well.

From here all the way back to Rainbow Park where I'd passed a half hour before—a good mile and a half—a brownfield now covers the land left from the dismantlement and demolition of US Steel's South Shore plant, once a behemoth mill works that employed in its heyday over twenty thousand steelworkers, many from nearby neighborhoods. In the foreground there's more upturned dirt mixed with rubble, but amid stands of weeds and scrub in the background rise giant walls of concrete, creat-ing parallel alleys the size of football fields where the giant furnaces once stood along with machinery that poured molten steel into great molded sheets. The ruins are striking in a sculptural sense: the size and hue of the concrete walls somehow brings out the texture of the grasses and cotton-wood trees in the distance by the lakeshore. Officially unused, the area and the mill's protected port have now become by default a fishing spot as well as an interesting place to hike and birdwatch.

Ahead I can see rusted steel towers, fifty or sixty feet high, whose pur-pose I cannot surmise, but they're obviously too costly for the city to dis-mantle. Perhaps because I've been observing infrastructure still in use all day, in the remnants of this steel plant I see something more than rusted steel and old concrete. To me, these ruins evoke all that has been lost in the lives of those who built families and businesses in these neighborhoods.

Not far from where I'm walking is another abandoned steelworks, Republic Steel. Here, in 1937, hired security forces beat hundreds of strik-ing steelworkers from Republic Steel, killing ten and wounding scores more. Dorothy Day, the indefatigable chronicler of America's exploita-tion of the poor, compared the slaughter of striking workers in Chicago to the horrors unfolding at the same time in Nazi Germany, fascist Italy, and Stalinist Russia: "We are sickened by stories of brutality in Germany and Russia and Italy . . . And here in America, last month, there was

a public exhibition of such brutality that the motion-picture film, taken by a Paramount photographer in a sound truck, was suppressed by the company for fear that it would cause riots and mass hysteria, it was so unutterably horrible." Like Haymarket in the West Loop, this historic site of the Memorial Day Massacre here on the South Side is little known and off the tourist grid, marked now by a small plaque a block or so away.

The city hopes that this two-mile lakefront brownfield will finally become useful once again with the construction of a microtechnology campus, anchored by a quantum computer operations center, which supposedly will attract other interested high-tech businesses. The city has already laid streets and sidewalks to entice developers. For all the hype and hope for an extension of the lakefront and a use for the ruins of the steel mill, it's clear that the city aims to do here what it has done elsewhere—create an anchoring urban renewal project to attract young professionals and redevelop the area. How people in the neighboring community will benefit is unclear. But in any case, for the city and the developers, first there's the little problem of the decades of slag and seeping toxic waste buried in the ground and dumped offshore.

Calumet River to East Side

Ahead there's another threshold to cross, another of the region's geo-graphical features so transformed by industrial shipping and toxic pol-lution that it's a stretch to even call this widened stream through what was once a vast wetland a river. I've arrived at Chicago's port and the entrance to its waterways, otherwise known as the much-maligned Cal-umet River. As the largest inland port in the US, the Calumet functions as a conduit moving massive amounts of raw materials into and out of the region as well as carrying away tons of industrial waste and storm runoff from the streets and highly contaminated soils of the surround-ing area.

Originally, the Calumet River was little more than a stream that flowed from Lake Calumet, which once was a grand inland lake and a remnant of the much larger, ancient Lake Chicago, the geological forbearer of Lake Michigan. Over the years, Lake Calumet, like so much of this area, has been sacrificed to industry and Chicago's mountains of waste. Lake Calu-met itself has shrunk to half of its pre-settlement size. For decades, com-mercial landfill enterprises accepted anything and everything for a price, and what couldn't be recycled—autos, trucks, railcars, appliances, con-struction debris—got dumped into Lake Calumet.

Like Lake Calumet, the system of waterways and rivers that have come to define this industrial region—the Calumet, the Grand Calumet, the Little Calumet, the man-made Indiana Canal—have all been severely poi-soned by industrial and municipal waste, not to mention being reversed, straightened, and obstructed. These waterways are not quite the ruins of rivers they once were before the establishment of the Environmental Pro-tection Agency and the passage of the Clean Water Act in the 1970s. Still the Calumet River system and waterways of Indiana regularly top the EPA's list of Areas of Concern.

Here toxic waste has settled to the bottom from over a century of indus-trial pollution, creating a thick sludgy soup of PCBs, toxic metals, and other pollutants. The Army Corps of Engineers and a variety of regional and governmental agencies continue to search for possible ways to dredge these dead zones where not even sludge worms can survive. But as with so many of America's severely polluted waterways, landfills, and former industrial sites, what prevents proper and effective restoration is not the issue of how to do it but rather the problem of cost and, most critically, where to dump the accumulations of toxic waste dredged from them.

Here I can see the fate of the river, as storage facility after storage facility and mountain after mountain of coal, scrap, and salt line the banks. Raw materials, grain, chemicals, oil, coke and slag, and God knows what else have passed through these waterways over the years, though it goes generally unnoticed except by those who live along and near the Calumet. Residents who live near the river must contend with a compounding stew of carcinogenic chemicals and toxins, not to mention soils contaminated by a century or more of indiscriminate and unregulated dumping. Here and on the Southwest Side people who live near the river report frequent soot on their cars and windows as well as black specks on food while eating in their backyards, particularly on windy days. After walking all day along the lakefront and then through South Side neighborhoods, mile by mile, I realize that the exploitation that holds up the city becomes more exposed as you move south from the Loop. In some places, like the former grounds of the South Works I've just passed, the craven and cruel cut-and-run ethic is incontrovertible. Peggy Salazar, of the Southeast Side Environmental Task Force, minces no words when she describes her Southeast Side community: "We have labeled ourselves the sacrifice zone because everything that nobody wants anywhere else in the city gets placed here."

And yet, to the west, arcing high over the river like a black rainbow of steel, the Chicago Skyway, a monument of human ingenuity and metalworking, elevates my mood. From the ground, I marvel at its size, the city's largest bridge, and before it the equally magnificent railroad bridge, now no longer in use. Both hang there above the river and the land some one hundred and fifty feet up, skeletons that go unexamined and underappreciated even as you drive over or by them, as I have done scores of times.

The drawbridge before me presents a kind of architectural wonder of its own, as all trestles, drawbridges, and old bridges made of steel or iron do for me. These structures invite the mind to see more than just a man-made crossing for vehicles from one side of a river to the other. These large skeletal creations somehow reverse the way I see. They are naked and unadorned, usually black and free of excess. They reveal an essential pattern, reminding me of the simplicity and exquisite order that undergirds both the built and natural environment. Or maybe my admiration of

these structures of engineering reminds me of how much my father liked photographing them, stopping along highways on family road trips and finding just the right view to capture their grand arcing form against the backdrop of the flatlands of the Midwest.

In the late afternoon light, the water is now midnight blue, churning and rocking against the rusted pilings and concrete embankments. Along the banks, cottonwood saplings and weeds branch out of the broken concrete and sour earth. Bits of plastic and trash swirl in the bubbles of brown scum, collecting in eddies as they drift under this magnificent work of steel and engineering. And though I'm falling far behind schedule, I wouldn't mind if a boat forced this truss bridge to rise so that I could watch it unfold from horizontal to vertical and back again.

These steel bridges and trestles played a monumental role not only in the history of steelmaking but also in Chicago's rise, quite literally, from its muddy, clogged streets of the late nineteenth century to the architectural wonder it became in the twentieth. Steel's qualities allowed engineers to imagine new uses for this lighter, more flexible metal that was still as sturdy and durable as iron. If steel could be used successfully to construct bridges, architects speculated that a similar frame structure could support multi-story buildings. With the construction of Chicago's Home Insurance Building, a ten-story building held aloft by a frame of steel, the modern skyscraper was born.

Looking at the constructed environment around me and back toward the city, I think again of the hands and bodies of the workers who have built everything I've passed since I walked out of my apartment this morning. The metaphor coined by Carl Sandburg's classic poem "City of Big Shoulders" is still an apt description of those legions of workers, men and women who continue to build and uphold the city's ethic of hard work. It's such an obvious observation on one level, but it reminds me of how shallow and superficial our perceptions can be of what creates and sustains urban life. By walking I'm learning that I'm discovering a city that my mind has mapped with fragmentary observations, glances out windows, narrow political viewpoints, and second- and third-hand impressions. Neighborhood by neighborhood, mile by mile, I'm struck at how easily we can build our beliefs about what afflicts our cities if over time our habits of seeing are based on routines and routes that bypass and thus erase whole sections of a city and the historic contributions of those who still live there.

Crossing the river takes me into my seventeenth Chicago neighborhood, known as the East Side. This corner of the city along Indiana's border and the Calumet River was, until recently, heavily populated by Eastern European immigrants who flocked to Chicago and the industrial region of Indiana at the turn of the century to work in the steel mills, factories, and meatpacking plants. Since the 1920s Mexican Americans have congregated in these working-class neighborhoods in the Calumet area on both sides of the border as well as many other neighborhoods throughout greater Chicago. Those of Latin descent now compose over 28 percent of Chicago's population, totaling 820,000, making Latinos the second largest ethnic group in Chicago, surpassing African Americans. Across the border in Lake County, Indiana, the number of Latinos continues to rise as well, currently at 94,000 out of a population of 490,000. In the Greater Chicago metropolitan area, the Latino population is well over 1,400,000.

Once over the river, I pass a scrap yard, partially hidden by fencing, that extends along the river out to its mouth and along the lakeshore.

I stop and step up on a concrete wall to look out at the piles of cubed scrap, formerly automobiles or perhaps appliances—I can't tell. The scrap industry was once seen as a dirty business that found a home near industrial areas with polluted brownfields and dumps. These days, the scrap and recycling business is huge. Here, along the shores of Lake Michigan, where more steel is made than perhaps anywhere else in North America, scrap has almost exclusively replaced raw iron ore in steelmaking. Across the street, behind a chain-link fence, a tugboat sits on blocks along with a row of beached sailboats discolored with age. Crossing another set of multiple railroad tracks, I see clearly just how congested this transport hub once was, and still is. Then, with little to no buffer from the trains and the highly contaminated industrial landscape, I'm back among those familiar two- and three-story brick flats of Chicago.

As I walk down uneven sidewalks, I find that this block of homes provides a good example of the city's historic project of raising up its streets and sidewalks out of the city's swampy origins so as to build a desperately needed sewer system below, forcing some homeowners to turn second floors into main entrances. In one sunken yard, weeds have taken over except inside a rough circular fence, maybe ten or fifteen feet in diameter. Within this makeshift waist-high fence of black, plastic sheeting, I can see tomatoes ready to pick, beans, and a patch of corn. The house next door, almost flush with the sidewalk, has a skinny porch no more than a yard wide with a freshly painted red wrought-iron fence. In these sunken spaces, impossible to see from a passing car, I note the splashes of color from geraniums blooming out of large tin cans, blood-red roses, hibiscus, and to my surprise, branches of bougainvillea intertwining around a side fence. Looking up, too, I find surprises. Above a storefront, in second-story windows, someone has taped posters of their favorite icons for all who pass below. Framed in weathered wood, there's Our Lady of Guadalupe, and next to her, The King himself, Elvis Presley.

On a street corner across from me, I spot the classic globe of a Schlitz Brewing Company sign above the door of an old tavern. These ornamental signs made of stamped steel can still be found all over the upper Midwest, and like this one, many have been painted over as this favorite beer lost out to the big breweries. But when I see them, hidden by paint, overshadowed by the neon lights of the popular brands of our age, I am reminded of those days when bars in both cities and small towns, like the one my grandfather owned, not only served alcohol but also functioned as union halls, voting stations, funeral parlors, and homes for the widowed and elderly, not to mention study halls where kids like my mother did homework while waiting for their parents to get off work.

Fittingly, on the next corner there's a brightly painted yellow-and-red hot dog stand, Skyway Dogs. Here, you could get your Polish sausage in the evening and admire the Skyway arching over the neighborhood and the city to the west with the sun setting behind it.

This lively corner of taverns, burrito shops, bodegas, and day-care centers near Calumet Park serves as the center of this largely Latino community, just as it once did for the East Europeans. The park isn't far off—in fact, I can see large trees and the entrance a half a block away. "The Little Lakefront," as those in this corner of the city call this park, is also made from landfill and rests on the southeasternmost point of Chicago. Although kept free of industrial and commercial use to give the thousands of workers and their families who live in this neighborhood a place to enjoy their Sunday outings, there's no escaping the pollution from the mills, the Indiana Toll Road, and BP's nearby refinery. Today,

though heavily used and a welcome retreat for those who live far from the lakefront, Calumet Park offers an uninspiring view of Indiana's industrial shore and all its belching smokestacks.

As the summer evening begins, Calumet Park is the place to be, and I can see families encamped under the tall oaks and elms, cars cruising around, throngs of children and baseball games. Chicagoans know that summer is short and every evening is to be savored for its warmth and society, but those who've come recently from Mexico and Latin America seem to have a connoisseur's feel for how to make every summer evening a kind of celebration of life.

Ahead, above a store front, a sign advertises PIZZA CARRY-OUT. When I get to the sign, I stop before a ripped screen door and peer inside. Towering over the ramshackle three-flats and corner bars stand the concrete pillars holding up the Indiana Toll Road. I can wait a little longer before celebrating a bit myself, as passing under the toll way a few hundred feet ahead, I'll officially leave the city of Chicago and the state of Illinois and be, as the song promises those of us who've left it, "back home again in Indiana."

IV

INTO INDIANA

Not I, nor any one else can travel that road for you,
You must travel it for yourself.
It is not far . . . it is within reach,
Perhaps you have been on it since you were born, and did not know,
Perhaps it is everywhere on water and on land.

—WALT WHITMAN, FROM SONG OF MYSELF

Indiana/Illinois State Line to Hammond, Indiana

I enter Indiana by descending into the earth, as I follow my shoreline high-way under a defunct railroad bed and the pillars of the Indiana Toll Road. What's left of a decrepit viaduct appears to be held together by its last coat of paint. The railroad bed has eroded into an earthen mound and out of the tracks man-sized weeds and sunflowers blooms. In the road beside me, cars slow to a crawl as they bounce over craters or weave around fallen chunks of this concrete cave. To avoid the pigeon shit that covers the nar-row walkway, I, too, must slow my pace as I steady myself on the equally slimy walls. But at least the tunnel provides a break from the heat.

In the last mile, I've witnessed the artifacts of America's transportation system, generation upon generation, corroding all around me—from side-walks to roadbeds, bridges to railroads. I'm enthralled by what I've never really bothered to see—the pathos of rust and ruins. Here, passing from Chicago's South Side into Hammond, is a world that's been left to itself, off in the corner and out of the way, except for those who live here and travel through these streets and over these bridges every day.

Emerging back into the dusty gold late afternoon light, I pass a tank that the patriotic town fathers of Hammond placed to create a triangular war memorial that bisects Indianapolis Boulevard and US 41. The tank points its barrel at Chicagoans slinking back with their full tanks of cheap gas, liquor, and cartons of cigarettes to avoid the city's sin taxes. Chicagoans pour over the border to play the slots at Northwest Indiana's casinos, too, where they contribute millions to Indiana's state coffers. But the barrel of that tank has come to represent for me another cross-state exchange that exacts a much deadlier cost on the families and neigh-borhoods of Chicago as well as those in Indiana. The defiant Indiana State Legislature refuses to recognize the public health disaster spreading across neighborhoods on either side of the state line due in large part to the proliferation of guns on the streets as a direct result of Indiana's lax gun laws.

An old man, overdressed in a long, thick, tattered gray coat, staggers down into the underpass as I walk up. When he reaches out from under his coat to ask for some change, I instinctively drop my eyes to the crum-bling sidewalk, my fingers in my pocket pinching coins that he obviously needs more than I do. A bad omen, I think. So, I turn back to offer him what I have, for my safe passage, but he's disappeared into the darkness heading back into Chicago.

It's hard to imagine a less likely place for a park than underneath the Indiana Toll Road, but as I make my way into Hammond, there's a concrete slab with two steel park benches, a trash can, and a withering row of tangled shrubs in a cozy corner, inviting me to take a break under this canopy of concrete. If I weren't dazed from low blood sugar and panicked about how I'm ever going to cover eight more miles to the edge of Gary before nightfall, I'd park myself down and marvel at the sheer wonder of life under an expressway. I mean, when do you have a chance to study, from this angle, such sculptures of concrete and rebar, and the engineering of something as massive as an expressway with pillars the size of a redwood tree trunk? And the roar! Like a waterfall of noise and exhaust flowing down on top of you. The wheels and tons of weight pound each time an eighteen-wheeler bounces by overhead, shaking the ground so much that I can feel the vibrations coming up into my groin and belly. Nonstop. Never ending. Billions of tons going east, billions going west, day after day, year after year.

Suddenly, from under the concrete and steel lattice and over the trees of heaven, their branches drooping like palm fronds, darts a squadron of birds. Wingless, it seems, they rocket in loose formation out over the evening traffic, dipping and diving around billboards and over the tops of houses. What are they? Pigeons? Not likely—they're too sleek and swift. As two more jet by, I take out my binoculars and nearly jump out into traffic to get a better look. Could they be? Yes, they are the famed feral green monk parakeets of the South Side! These parrots have increased significantly over the years as they have learned to adapt to Chicago's cold winters by foraging feeders and holing up in their enormous communal nests made of sticks. One of their first and most famous colonies was outside the apartment of the late former mayor Harold Washington on 51st Street in Hyde Park, which the mayor proudly pointed to as a sign of changing times in Chicago. But no one knows exactly how they got here or what their effects might be down the road on other birds and the environment.

My next challenge is to cross the highway. But where? Cars shoot down the off ramp of the tollway, barreling by over my shoulder as I walk alongside, making it hard to think. Fortunately, I spot a traffic light a few hundred yards ahead, and it makes all six lanes stop for half a minute, allowing this endangered species walking on two legs to scurry across.

I recall how once I tried to ford a river of motorbikes, cars, bikes, and rickshaws in Chennai, India, with luggage no less, thinking surely I could make it across a road no wider than my neighborhood street to check in to my hotel—but in the end I had to walk down the road and wait with everyone else at a light that stopped traffic only every ten minutes for the crowd to hustle across before the dam burst open again. Worldwide, according to the United Nations, 22 percent of all traffic deaths reported each year—some 1.35 million people—are the result of motorists hitting pedestrians.

Motivated by hunger and thirst, my sights are set on those golden arches happily lit up ahead, over the empty lots and the brake and muffler shop. I'm partial to McDonald's. Why, I don't really know. Fifty years of French fries might have something to do with it, give or take a few years living abroad—where, I must admit, I have found myself in line on the Champs Elysees stuttering out in my best bad French, "Un grand milk-shake et pommes frites, s'il vous plait."

When McDonald's came to my hometown of Marion, Indiana, in 1967, there was a palpable sense of pride. Our factory town of thirty thousand souls had entered American middle-class luxury, so we believed. The future had finally arrived: frozen foods, moonshots, color TV, and fast food. Those days of the downtown diners (one of which my aunt owned) were done. Who wanted a tenderloin as big as your face, or pie that someone actually made from scratch and served with ice cream from the town creamery? We begged my dad to just drive by the new McDonald's erected on the city's booming bypass so that we could peer into the glowing, florescent-lit miracle.

At the counter, there's a Latino family ordering via their teenage daughter, who, along with the counter girl, switches from Spanish to English to Spanglish. But I'm just happy to be inside with air-conditioning; after all, I'm the foreigner, as Hammond is home to yet another wave of Chicagoland's immigrant story, with nearly half of its population now from Mexico or Central America. I settle for a benign fish combo with a chocolate shake, and of course an order of large fries.

As soon as I collapse into a chair, my legs feel like sandbags pouring out onto the floor. The bottoms of my feet burn. I stare for a few moments at my food, the starchy display boxed and bagged, ready to eat. Then, the next thing I know, I'm shaking the box of fries for every last crumb and sucking up the final straw full of sucrose. Blissfully buzzed by sugar and carbohydrates, I think of putting my head down on the table, but know I'd better not risk it.

Instead, I stare out the wide windows at the industrial landscape of Hammond, Indiana. "The City in the Middle of It All," a sign proclaims in the median of Indianapolis Boulevard, the mayor's name beneath. Indeed, Hammond is in the middle of one of the most concentrated industrialized zones in America. Here, the famed corporate giants process, forge, and belch in every direction: Cargill, Unilever, BP, Cleveland Cliffs, US Steel, Union Carbide and many more—along with miles of tank farms. (And that's only what I can see.) On the other side of the highway, three squad cars have cornered a man in his van in front of a shuttered cigarette outlet. Behind this silent drama, double-decker containers on several railroad tracks await their next load, a reminder of the area's historic role in the railroad business—once almost every major rail line in America passed through here. Many of the railcars are tagged with colorful signatures of protest, a night's work for graffiti artists along the routes of post-industrial mid-America. Beyond the wall of artwork, where the lake should be, the brick bastion of State Line Power Company once stood, spewing forth from its coal-burning furnaces until it was finally shut down for its notorious violations of the EPA's Clean Air Act. Indiana only recently met federal EPA Clean Air Act standards, making it one of the last states to comply with an act passed in 1970.

But what catches my eye now is the webbing of electrical lines and the towers that carry them, appearing like giant black praying mantises on their hind legs marching off into the marshlands behind me. Why haven't I noticed before how these towers dominate this landscape? How magnificent they seem from the ground: geometric patterns of steel girders against the fading pale light, stretching over the distillery towers and the churches ahead in the neighboring city of Whiting. How am I seeing this all for the first time when I've passed by here scores of times before? Is it my fatigue that has illuminated these landscapes I once viewed as unworthy of my attention? Or has walking all day shifted my perception, opening my senses to a parallel world that exists only for those who enter by foot?

Hammond to Whiting, Indiana

Standing up from my plastic seat, I must hold on to the table to support my exhausted leg muscles. Not a good sign. But I march on, dutifully dumping my tray of trash in the bin, and push myself back outside into the thick, hot Indiana air. I've been in McDonald's for maybe twenty minutes, but as soon as I step outside, I can see that I will have to contend not only with muscle fatigue but also with what I've purposely ignored from the outset—time.

Daylight is clearly on the wane as the sun has dipped to just above Hammond's skyline of churches and electrical towers. It's clear that I'm not going to make it through Whiting and East Chicago to arrive at Gary's Majestic Star casino on the lakefront before dark. But do I stop to check my map? Do I count the miles and make some new calculation? No. After a full day of movement, rationality holds little sway. All I know to do is keep walking. I'm off, noticing the trash on the side of the road and wondering how many years ago it landed there, buried as it is by soot, weeds, and a crop of hybrid cattail.

The layers of trash make me think of the first Earth Day of 1970 and how it influenced me and so many young people. Planting trees at school and picking up trash along the highways were small things, I suppose, but the idea that there was an environment and that its health depended on humans was wholly new. My friends and I were so inspired that we decided to pick up trash along a highway not far from my house, State Road 37, a major route through Indiana. But we managed no more than a couple hundred yards before we had filled up our garbage bags. Motorists honked and we felt like heroes, but I remember how sobering it was to see the layers of trash in the dirt and realize that it didn't disappear somehow, as I had thought or was led to believe, but instead kept adding up, and that all the people in my own town—my dad, me, my friends, everybody—were collectively responsible. As I think about this odd memory of decades past, something comes flying out the window of what looks like a late-model, beat-up Oldsmobile, and along with it a guttural spew of words I can't make out. Interesting that I've walked through supposedly dangerous neighborhoods on Chicago's far South Side without any harassment, but now in Indiana I'm a target of derision. The roadside is wide, but for the first time I feel the danger not just of errant cans and litter but also of those who sit behind the wheel of thousands of pounds of steel.

Though the sugars and starch gave me a boost, my legs feel heavier than before I sat down, like I'm wading through sand or marshy grass—which I would be if I'd been here one hundred and fifty years before. Miles and miles of a vast open marsh still dominate Northwest Indiana, however, despite landfills and the building of railroads and expressways.

As if I need to be reminded that I'm heading toward the great fountain from which flows the Midwest's lifeblood of unleaded gasoline, there in the foreground of BP's distillery towers, a mile or so away, is a brand new, thirty-two-pump BP gas station. When BP bought Amoco, it decided to rebrand itself as "Beyond Petroleum," changing the name on its hundreds of newly acquired gas stations across the Midwest. (Interestingly now the company is rebranding again, bringing back the Amoco logo to lure the older crowd and fool those outraged by BP's Deepwater oil spill of 2010)

Passing the BP gas station, my dirt path along the road thins. For a couple hundred more feet I fight through chest-high weeds, then the road-side becomes more walkable as I make my way under a hundred-foot-high gigantic horseshoe, lit with red and gold lights, advertising Hammond's Horseshoe Casino to all buzzing along the tollway. Suddenly, the trashy roadside and marshlands are replaced by a concrete ramp with a flowing fountain surrounded by perfectly manicured grass and a ring of flowering plants. I could pull in here myself and, for only $150, have all I want to eat at the buffet, play the slots, and quit while I'm ahead. But I've already booked my room at the Majestic Star and I convince myself it won't be that far now that I've made it to Hammond.

Next on my path along Indianapolis Boulevard is the sprawling home of one of Cargill's processing facilities, its front offices nestled on the woody shores of what remains of another of the many shallow wetland lakes along Indiana's shore. Like Lake Calumet and Wolf Lake, Lake Hyde has shrunk as landfills have incrementally added more land for industrial use. Across from Cargill on corporate row is Unilever's subsidiary, Dove Soap. In this hulking, mustard-colored processing plant, vast amounts of palm oil shipped from Indonesia are blended with other chemicals to make creamy bars of soap. Though it may seem benign to us as we shower, these bars of scented soap come at a cost to the rainforests and peoples of Indonesia and beyond. Unilever, like other major agribusinesses in Indonesia, have historically been responsible for cutting and burning of rainforests and, more indirectly, political instability. The smoke from the rainforest fires creates serious air quality problems for farmers and peasants, and massive clouds of it float into mainland cities in Southeast Asia, causing alarming levels of pollution, not to mention adding millions of tons of particulate matter and carbon to the atmosphere.

Along this street stretches the world of greater Chicago, home to thousands upon thousands who no longer work exclusively in heavy industry but now also in any number of other sectors of the Chicago economic hub. Hammond extends far to the west, where it borders Chicago's southwestern suburbs. One after another, I pass classic worker cottages, mixed in with brick bungalows and two-story houses, each using up just enough space to have a bit of a yard front and back along with a one-car garage. Some have that familiar sunken side yard with a neat little garden, a row of rose bushes by the house, marigolds along the walkway to the garage, and, enshrined by a half-buried, antique porcelain bathtub, a pale blue ceramic statue of the Virgin Mary.

On every other corner is the traditional neighborhood bar, each ornamented with an Old-Style Beer sign glowing white and blue, a Chicago Blackhawks logo on the door, and, depending on the clientele or the owner's preference, either a Cubs or Sox logo as well. I pass one bar that's open so I can see a couple of guys hunched over their half-filled glasses of beer as a TV screen beams the image of a fluorescent green baseball field somewhere in North America. I stop and look longingly inside. Taverns still are safe havens of a sort for the traveler, open to all for a drink and a place to rest. But I keep going, knowing that if I go in and have one beer, my pilgrimage will end there on one of those old stools.

Ahead I see a Walgreens. The familiar red-lit logo beckons as dusk falls over Whiting's brick churches and corner businesses and, as it is designed to do, triggers in me a learned response: *Do I need anything?*

In Whiting, according to my plan to hug the coast as much as possible, my route will turn toward the lake and take a public road through the refinery. There I'll pass Mark Town, the historic worker's community, and then continue past another US Steel Tin plant on into the neighborhoods of East Chicago.

The closer I get to Walgreens, as I walk through the tidy streets of Whiting, the more my mind becomes fixated on the cool air and goodies inside. So, instead of thinking about making my turn at the major intersection that leads to Mark Town, I head through the doors of Walgreens.

Inside, in no time, I find myself walking aimlessly down one aisle and up the next as if drugged by the bright packaging and cool air. I finger bars for breakfast, bars for power, bars for protein. For a while I look at hats, t-shirts, and underwear. Before a newsstand, I kneel and read the headlines of the local paper, the *Northwest Times*, like I've been lost for days in a forest wondering what I may have missed. I touch different sized bags and flavors of potato chips. I stare into the refrigerated case at cartons of milk. With three plastic bags of supplies—sports drinks, candy bars, gum, and a memory chip for my camera—I walk back out into the evening heat.

Out of habit, I stride into the parking lot and without the slightest hesitation head toward the lone parked car. Halfway across the lot, I freeze. *Where's my car?* Seized by panic, I turn fully around looking for my Ford Escort until I finally awaken to where I am and what I'm doing.

Even with the skies over Whiting glowing from BP's refinery, dusk has turned to darkness while I was waylaid inside Walgreens. For a moment, I don't move or think, aware of just how disoriented my mind has become from walking so far. I put down my pack, stuff in my purchases, and swing it onto my sweat-soaked back. Chastened, I march out of the parking lot, pumping my arms and pushing my legs to move as fast as they can toward a blinking stoplight I can see in the distance. For the first time, I feel some strange sense of fear.

Hanging down from the city's turn-of-the-century streetlamps are banners that read "Welcome to Whiting," and in homage to the city's benefactor, in small green print over the top, "Refining Our Community." Indeed, BP is doing just that, and at a rate that only a handful of refineries in the world can match—some 400,000 plus barrels a day, nearly all extracted from the deposits of oil sands under the boreal forests of northeastern Alberta.[1]

---

1   BP's purchase of Amoco (Standard Oil of Indiana) was a strategic move, as the company foresaw what was coming literally down the pipeline with the development of the tar sand fields in Alberta. The transnational behemoth knew that there were few refineries able to handle this bonanza of bitumen-rich, very dirty oil. So even as BP was slyly redefining itself as a "new energy company" with its name change and PR campaign to promote itself as "Beyond Petroleum," it was also reconstructing Whiting's hundred-year-old refinery on Lake Michigan to process the tar sand.

East toward the lake, rising over this city out of the toxic goo that has seeped into the sandy soil from a century of dumping by not only Rockefeller's Standard Oil of Indiana but also a slew of other oil companies, stands the lone survivor: British Petroleum's flagship refinery for North America on the shores of Lake Michigan. Huddled there next to it, the city of Whiting holds on. Except for Whiting, the three other industrial cities of Northwest Indiana have precipitously declined since the 1960s. While Whiting's population has held steady at 5,000, neighboring East Chicago has lost nearly half of its residents, dropping from 55,000 in 1960 to 26,370 in 2020. Gary's population has dwindled even further, from around 180,000 in 1960 to nearly a third at less than 70,000, while Hammond's population fell from 112,000 to 78,000.

What difference does it make that the sun has set, since I'm walking in the orange glow of dozens of distillery towers lit from top to bottom, with flames of gas shooting into the carbon-rich skies over Northwest Indiana? In my big plans of days before, I was hoping this would be the highlight of my walk, or at least one of the highlights on my way to the late great

dunes of Indiana. But now, I'm just hoping I can keep it together to get to the casino and to bed.

Despite my state of mind and fatigue, I press on to the next stoplight, but as I look ahead, something isn't right. I'm heading for a T in the road, and this doesn't gel with the map I have in my mind. I obviously need to turn right, toward the lake, and pass through the refinery. But this wasn't the route I took in my car the day before. Did I take a wrong turn someplace? Where am I?

Too panicked to remember that I can just open my compact foldable phone and check GPS, instead I drop my pack on the side of the road to get out one of my maps. But in the dimness, and with all the shit I've stuffed into it, I can't find anything. It would have been smart to pack a flashlight, but I stupidly didn't imagine I'd be walking past sunset. After feeling around and finding nothing, in a burst of frustration I upend the pack right there on the gravel: pens, keys, extra batteries, notebooks, underwear, and all the rest lie in a heap at my feet, including my plastic bags from Walgreens where I could have actually bought something worth stopping for, like a flashlight. And among it all, there's no map. Not only did I not bother to stick a flashlight in with all these useless things, I also managed to forget three separate maps—along with my fucking brains, apparently—back in my apartment.

British Petroleum's Refinery, Whiting, to East Chicago, Indiana

For a moment I just stand there with my hands on my hips, looking at my pack and then down the road lined with oil depots. I realize that having no map is not the problem; the problem is that I've still too far to walk and I'm unable to think clearly. If I had any sense at all, I'd head back toward Hammond and find a cab to take me to some Super 8 or Motel 6, call it a day and start fresh the next morning. But pride and extreme fatigue win out over rational decision-making. I pick up my gear, cross the road at the light, and head into the bright lights of BP's refinery.

Crossing four railroad tracks, I pass Happy Jack Liquors and a row of wooden houses near BP's gates, wave to an old man sitting on his porch smoking a cigarette, and hope I'm heading in the right direction. Behind the row of houses, ten-thousand-gallon oil depots, their crowns lit with cherry-red blinking lights like giant cupcakes, extend, one behind the other, into the humid, oily darkness. Ahead are more depots and a clean, well-lit field station, all behind a ten-foot chain-link fence.

On the other side of the highway, encased in pipes and scaffolding, dozens of distillery towers stand like a gargantuan flaming pipe organ against the darkened skies over Lake Michigan. From the ground, it feels as if I've entered some science-fiction fantasy land dreamed up by Dr. Seuss: pipes four abreast snake along the ground and then disappear into the brown sandy earth or bend at right angles and cross the road overhead. Amazingly, an employee in bright green jogging shorts takes off down the sidewalk, apparently out for his evening run, making me feel a bit better about what I might be breathing. But it can't be healthy to work, let alone exercise, in a place where workers are warned as they enter by blinking digital signs: DO NOT BRING IN LIGHTERS OR CIGARETTES. One match and me, the jogger, and the guy on the porch could be blown to bits along with those on the night shift. I'm aware, as those who live and work around this facility should be, of the company's history of explosions and deadly accidents. Not only was BP responsible for the eleven workers whose bodies were never found on its offshore drilling platform in the Gulf in 2010, but in 2005 its lax safety standards caused a massive explosion at its refinery in Texas City, Texas, that killed fifteen workers and injured some 170 others. Two years after the incident in Texas City, OSHA found that the oil giant had not corrected its violations and still had seven hundred safety hazards, resulting in the stiffest penalty ever handed down by the federal agency against a corporation.

From up close the distillery towers no longer appear as hazardous and horrific, but instead trigger my boyhood fascination with the mechanics and chemistry of oil refining. What's taking place here in this surreal landscape along the lake? Whether one is a child or an adult, the process of turning fossilized plant matter into gasoline, asphalt, polyesters and paint, solvents and kerosene, jet fuel and any number of other products can capture the imagination. Who wants to imagine the degradation of forests, or ecosystems millions of years in the making being ripped open by bulldozers bigger than a two-story house, when one can instead try to fathom how engineers can design machines to hoover up tar sand and send it along thousands of miles of pipelines with just the right mix of chemicals to keep it flowing, under rivers and even along the floor of Lake Michigan? Here, in this sci-fi fantasy come to life, these rocket-like distillery towers before me boil a stew of ancient sea creatures and trees at 800 degrees Fahrenheit and miraculously filter out the impurities to make regular, premium, and super unleaded for you and me to buy and burn.

A teenage Black boy rides by on his bike and then in the other direction a white girl, their bikes like horses in a pastoral scene of ages ago. Allies, I think, as they glide by, their bodies floating over the road, their legs pumping through air thickened by benzene and particulate matter. Both turn and glance back at me as they pass, in wonder, I imagine, at who might be walking with a backpack through their territory of teenage freedom. "To be is to be perceived," the metaphysician George Berkeley observed, and their acknowledgement lifts my spirit and sends me deeper into the edgelands of industrial Indiana.

The oil depots ended a few hundred yards back, and I'm now walking along a mysterious ten-foot-high wall of fire-proof material. Behind it, adding to the intrigue, stretches an earthen wall that parallels the fence. Yellow signs every couple of hundred feet read: WARNING, US GOVERNMENT, NO TRESPASSING.

At first, I think it's just another of the many Superfund sites that dot the region, which would explain the fence and the telltale pipes sticking up out of the top of the wall of dirt. But squinting far ahead, I can see a small bridge under two towering streetlights. And now I know where I am: I'm circumnavigating the home of thousands of tons of toxic sludge that the Army Corps of Engineering dredged up from the nearby Indiana Harbor and Ship Canal and then dumped here at this enclosed site. I'd seen this very hellhole from above the day before on Google Maps.

I stop as I reach the center of the bridge and look down into the brackish blackness of the canal twenty feet below. A snaking boom holds back a sudsy scum with bits of trash; behind it floats a sheen of oil. Thickets and trees hang over one side of the canal, and on the other there's another earthen wall to ensure, theoretically at least, that PCBs and other toxins won't leak into the canal. But the lights atop the wall reveal a drainage pipe emptying runoff of some kind directly back into the canal.

I walk across the highway to the other side, lean over the same crumbling concrete guardrail, and look down into the stagnant cesspool. As I slowly raise my head, I follow the canal as it extends in a straight line out to Lake Michigan. The huge, shadowy metal structures of the steelmakers stand along the shore, and next to them, barely visible, a towering crane. If there are any tankers below in the port, it's too dark to tell. But out over the lake, beyond the man-made gloom, twinkling stars remain free for those who may need to see them.

To the south and west, the sky has slowly turned from pinkish yellow to an ominous orange glow, making it appear as if there's a giant fire somewhere in the city behind me. In the distance, I can see the lights of the Indiana Toll Road crossing over Wolf Lake. From there, this landscape and all who try to survive in it have become invisible—pipes, depots, cattails, canals, tankers, teenagers on bicycles, all a mere blur if seen at all. But from the ground, from here in the middle of the stillness of the industrial night, I can feel the rawness of the earth. Barren but not dead, this land is still alive, and in its living there's something as real and wild as anywhere I've ever hiked. As I breathe, I can feel it seeping into my lungs and flesh and the ventricles of my heart. In its wildness the past is still very much alive, a reminder that nothing is forgotten or invisible. That destiny, as its Latin root "stinare" implies, comes from where one stands. And where am I standing? In some remote industrial no-man's-land far from human habitation? No, I'm standing within walking distance of where I live, work, and turn on my tap for water, along with ten million other people on the shores of this Great Lake.

Far ahead, I see a stoplight, a few random streetlights, and a hint here and there of homes and buildings. Walking quickly through an unruly stand of wild sunflowers growing out of the broken sidewalk, I make it over the bridge and out of the thicket surrounding the canal. On the other side, I'm greeted by a sign erected by the Lion's Club cheering me on into East Chicago. Incredibly, no more than a few hundred yards from the canal and the eventual storage site for its toxic sludge is not only a park with tennis courts and a par-three golf course but also East Chicago Central High School and a newly built middle school. At least two thousand students within a windy day's reach of a toxic dump site.

On the other side of the road, pipes belonging to another of the many energy conglomerates in the area, Buckeye Pipeline, run into the darkness along the canal, reminding me just how many pipelines crisscross this whole region, transporting oil into and out of BP and other oil companies. Enbridge's infamous Line 6A ends its cross-continental transport of thick bitumen from Alberta just a few miles away. Enbridge Line 6 Oil Pipeline is a major pipeline in the Canadian/US Enbridge Pipeline System, which carries petroleum from western Canada to eastern Canada by way of the Great Lakes states of Minnesota, Wisconsin, Illinois, Indiana, and Michigan. It consists of two separate lines, Line 6A and Line 6B, which begin and end in Griffith, Indiana, a few miles from Gary. The largest on-land oil spill in American history occurred in Line 6B when it ruptured in July 2010, spilling more than one million barrels into a tributary of the Kalamazoo River in Michigan.

Beside Buckeye is a fire station, which makes sense, and adjacent to it, making even more sense, is Lake County's Mental Health Clinic. For how are people supposed to manage their sanity when they must send their kids to schools surrounded by toxic waste sites?

Thankfully, I can see more lights and an intersection near the two schools. When I get to the traffic light, a black and white East Chicago squad car pulls out of the school parking lot and slowly passes me. A welcome sign, I think, planning to flag the car down and get clear directions, but then the scowl on the white officer's face as he peers through his window makes me realize what I probably look like: some lunatic in hiking shorts with a backpack coming out of the weeds and wasteland of BP. I put my head down as if I know where I'm going and hump it across the road toward a golden glowing Corona sign in the window of a taqueria.

Inside the taqueria four Latino men sit at a table with their bright yellow beer, chips, and salsa. Looking down the highway into the darkness of East Chicago, I wonder how far I have yet to walk to reach the casino and whether I should risk it despite not really knowing where I am. Then it begins to rain. Large drops precipitate out of the dense night air, splattering on the pavement, hitting my arms and legs, and streaking down my hot, dirty body. Another wave of fatigue hits me, and I lower myself slowly onto the concrete steps to sort out what to do: Keep walking? Flag down an errant cab? Ask the police for help? Break down and call a friend? I look back at the men through the window, enjoying their beers and fat burritos on the platters before them. Maybe they can help?

Here come the cops again. I jump up and put my cell phone to my ear in a panic, feigning my legitimacy for the police, pretending to be talking to someone on the phone. What will I say if they stop and ask me what I'm doing? Tell them I'm walking to the Indiana Dunes?

After twenty-eight miles, it's time to let go of my pride and call a cab to ferry me the last mile or so to the casino and my hotel. So, I call the Majestic Star Casino, hoping they have a shuttle. They don't, but they give me the number of some local cab companies. When I call the first number, a guy listens to me for a few seconds and then asks, "You're where?" When I repeat myself, he hangs up. The second tells me it'll take an hour and half, and the third hangs up as well.

I walk back to the stoop and slowly sit down. My hips ache, my legs buzz like they're still walking, my feet—to the extent I can feel them—seem like bones and joints floating in a skin sack of acid, my hair lies plastered against my skull. I stink.

For a few minutes I sit there and stare into the sickly glow in the northwestern sky over the land I've walked through for the last fourteen hours. I take out my cheap little cell phone and scroll through the names, contemplating which friend I could call at nearly ten o'clock on a Tuesday night. But I can't do it. It would be too awkward, too humiliating. I didn't even tell anyone about my insane idea for fear they'd talk me out of doing it.

Then, out of the darkness, a miracle: a cab with its lights on.

I run out almost into the middle of the road to force the cab to stop. The window comes down and a round-faced Black man shakes his head emphatically and, in a familiar francophone West African accent, dashes my hopes: "No, no, not open. I'm going home."

"But, but your light is on . . . " I plead as he shakes his head and rolls up his window. "Just to the casino?"

He speeds off.

I sit back down and decide to wait for the cops.

And they do come by, once, but in pursuit apparently of some other troubled souls. The taqueria dims its lights, and the men inside save me from any further humiliation by going out the back door. Here I sit, soaked in sweat, slumped like a sad kid on his porch stoop.

To rub it in, strangely, the same cab returns, still with its goddamn light on. Desperate, I stand up and wave him down again, thinking maybe he can call his dispatcher for me.

"I know, I know," I start, my voice breaking into a whine as he reluctantly stops again and rolls down his window. "I know you're going home, but I'm in trouble here, maybe you could call your dispatcher and they could possibly call someone to . . . "

"Okay, I will take you," and he waves his hand hurriedly for me to get in.

I can't believe I've heard him right, "Really? You'll take me?"

He nods, and I pull open the heavy door, nearly falling over because I'm so tired. But I right myself and tumble into the cavernous and blissfully cool back seat, hoping he'll not notice my near fall and think I'm a drunk on his way to one of the nearby casinos. Almost immediately I begin to lie down on the wide cushioned back seat, but bolt back up knowing I haven't yet told him where I'm going. "I'm going to the casino. I can't thank you, really, thank you so much, you won't believe me . . . " and I cut myself off, not wanting to jeopardize my ride. "The casino will be fine, thank you." Relieved, he nods and hits the gas and we're off.

"I saw you needed a ride," he says, turning down the BBC on his radio. "I'm sorry I didn't pick you up the first time. But I'm not allowed. Only have a license for Chicago. I thought you were maybe a set-up, maybe the police. I could get fined for picking up passengers outside of Chicago, you know?"

"No, no, no, I'm not the police," I say, laughing to myself.

We talk a bit about his work and how hard it is to make a living for cabdrivers these days, with Uber, the rise in gas prices, and endless numbers of parking and traffic tickets—thousands of dollars each year, he tells me.

"What do you do?" he asks, turning back to me.

"I'm a writer, a kind of journalist, and I'm doing this—this experiment. You probably won't believe me . . . " I pause and can't help myself, seeing his curious eyes and sincere face. "I know this will sound crazy to you, but I'm walking to the Indiana Dunes. The park, the sand dunes near Gary, you know? I've been trying to write a book, a book about walking."

"Where people swim—the big sand piles? Oh, yes. I've taken my family there once."

"Yeah, the dunes, I'm walking there."

"Where did you walk from?"

"Chicago."

"Chicago? Really?"

"Yes, I know . . . Can you believe it?"

"Walking?" He muses, chuckling, meeting my eyes in his rearview mirror. "Where I come from, I think everyone could write a book about walking."

Grinning and nodding, I lean and rest my arms on the back of the front seat. Somehow, I'm not surprised that out of the oily orange shadows of the night a West African has appeared to guide me to safety. Like a folk-tale, he's arrived to remind me of those lessons I'd learned while walking in Senegal years before. All day my mind had slid into reveries of those long walks I'd taken while working in the Peace Corps. I'm not sure if it was the feeling of the sun beating down on the back of my neck or if it was the length of time and the distance that triggered the memories, but there I was, tramping off into the sandy savannahs, heading out into the sun-bleached afternoons, making my way from village to village, passing those elephantine baobab and fanlike acacia on the horizons. Again and again, memories came to me, especially in the past hours as I'd made my way to the South Side where I'd arrived, heart-broken and haunted, after leaving Senegal.

In his chuckling laughter at me and my attempt to make a pilgrimage through this new home of his, I recalled the harsh realities of life in those farming villages where, indeed, walking was a daily routine and a neces-sity: the children off to schools miles away, walking into the heat and swirls of dust; the women with babies strapped to their backs, walking back and forth from wells balancing precious basins of water; the Fulani herdsmen among their boney cattle; the pilgrims and the migrant workers from Mali and Guinea. Walking there, indeed, was no pastime but a way of survival.

The Senegalese farmers nicknamed me "tukkikat," (the traveler) in the tongue of the Wolof, a moniker given to the restless, to the ones who find themselves forever on the road. They'd seen in me in a matter of months my character and stamped it on to me, with their nickname. And they were right.

In letters to me, I remember my friends and family often asked me what it was like living there in a mud-brick hut among the Wolof and Mandinka farmers and their families. I'd often say that it felt like being a character in folktale. By that I was trying to describe not only the day-to-day ways of life of rural people who lived within the rhythms of the land, where animate and inanimate were not separated, and like time itself, boundaries could not be fixed. Here, there was a sense that an act or deed mattered for all time, affecting the past as well as the future. My coming there, they'd told me, had long ago been ordained. And when I returned from walking off to another community to do my work, they thanked Allah for my return, as they did the rain and the bounty of their meager harvest of peanuts, so crucial to their welfare. To them, my coming had nothing to do with me or the magnanimity of America; no, I was there as a sign of their belief in the powers of their ancestors and their faith in the benevolence of Allah.

I learn that my taxi-driver is from Cote d'Ivoire and he'd immigrated a few years ago. His name is Gabriel. I'm not surprised either that he'd just moved to Indiana (Merrillville) from—where else—Rogers Park, where I'd begun my journey hours before, home to many immigrants who drive taxis for a living.

As he navigates through the industrial landscape of more oil depots and empty stretches of brownfields to find the casino outside of Gary, we become so involved in a discussion about oil spills and a massive dumping scandal back home in his hometown of Abidjan that we get lost, and I must get out and ask for directions at a White Castle back in Whiting. But he cancels the meter, and after more twisting and turning through East Chicago we come upon the pitch blackness of the lake and Donald Trump's old casino.

He's eager to talk, having been alone all day with only his radio for company. "I drive through now every day, coming back from Chicago, looking and wondering at this, this area, these cities with the poor people and broken buildings," he says, his hand directing my eyes to the darkened landscape before us. "I don't understand it. This is America. How can this be? I ask myself. I didn't think I'd find this when I came here. People living like this. I don't understand. What happened here?"

Majestic Star Casino, Gary, Indiana

After Gabriel drops me off at the casino, I find my second-floor hotel room, sink five dollars into a vending machine down the hall, peel off my soot and sweat soaked clothes, and draw a hot bath.[2] With salt and sugar in the form of a sixteen-ounce soft drink, I soak in a state of stupor until

---

2   The Majestic Star Casino closed in 2021. One of its gaming licenses was bought by another casino in Gary, Hard Rock Casino.

hunger forces me to resurrect myself out of the water and my room in search of real food at the casino.

I had envisioned a celebratory meal of several thousand calories at the casino's steakhouse, whose website advertised an outdoor patio overlooking the lake. Never mind that it was surely well past ten o'clock and that to reach my fantasy it would be necessary to walk yet another thousand feet or so to the casino. I put on a clean shirt and underwear and drag myself over a skyway that links the hotel to the casino complex.

Surprisingly my legs move without much pain, motivated I suspect by a growing fear that the steakhouse might close. Reaching the casino, I discover that the down escalator does not function, which forces me to do something I have not done all day—descend steps. So, with the mellow voice of Louis Armstrong being piped through the hallway and thoughts of eating a large pile of mashed potatoes, I slowly lower my aching body down each step, holding firmly to the railing, each knee bending with protest.

I make it into a large hall where ostentatious chandeliers give light to plum-colored walls trimmed in gold wainscoting. Prominently displayed on a wall for all to see are the jackpot winners at the slots for the past week: beaming faces framed in golden stars, all older women, their big winnings of as much as five hundred dollars posted below their photographs.

I follow three women down the hallway where I see a sign for the "Steak House," but when I get closer, I see the lights are dim and employees are vacuuming and setting up tables for the next day. As I had imagined, though, there is a patio with a view of Buffington Harbor and the glowing orange lights of Cleveland Cliffs steelworks across the water.

Feeling cheated, famished, and very tired but determined, I stop two more ladies coming down the hall. "Where can I get something to eat?"

"Oh, there's the grill," they respond, pointing ahead up another flight of stairs. "They've got stuff to eat."

I labor up a flight of stairs and, as the women promised, at the top is a grill by the name of "Wings N' Things." Slumping over Styrofoam plates of fried "things," tired-looking parties, done for the night, sit eating their meals mechanically in silence. Scanning the menu mounted over the grill leaves me uninspired, though the two chocolate doughnuts in a glass case at the counter look edible. I stagger on, determined to get at least a serious drink or two in one of the two ferry boats that house the casino.

Though gambling is marketed and mythologized as a high-risk game for bad boys, big spenders, and their female escorts, there is a long line of wheelchairs parked along the enclosed pier that leads into the ferryboats. It seems that what I'd heard about these casinos being largely surrogate bingo halls is not so far off. Increasingly, the gaming industry has become very effective in making its profits from repeat players with incomes of less than fifty thousand dollars who live near casinos. A study published in the *Christian Science Monitor* revealed that nearly 80 percent of the money lost in gambling come from this income group. The gaming industry overwhelming makes its money on people who spend small amounts playing slot machines. These computerized slot machines are designed to keep people playing, as they ingeniously offer small winnings to induce continued play. By having slots of as little as a penny, casinos entice people to play multiple machines for hours, losing what seems to them to be small amounts of money, but as they return again and again, often weekly, these players end up losing thousands of dollars each year.

I follow the lead of others and stand in a roped line to "check in" at the casino, but when I reach the woman at a round desk who checks us in, she waves me on through, as I'm not a regular. Regular casino-goers check in to turn in vouchers, while others must be checked against a list of people who are banned by the casinos because of debt or who must report themselves to all nearby casinos because of addiction problems. Before walking on board, I stop to read an official-looking placard warning of the financial and physical health risks of gambling. By law, Indiana's General Assembly requires that its ever-booming casino businesses post these warning signs; this one also informs the gambling public that this casino is donating "part" of its winnings (a mere fraction) to public health programs to help those who might fall victim to the ravages of a gambling addiction. Indeed, the risk of becoming addicted to gambling increases the closer you live to a casino. Once seen as scandalous and sinful by conservatives in the state, gambling in Indiana has followed the national trend as policymakers have realized that the gaming industry could ameliorate the problem of rising costs for state services in an economy struggling due to deindustrialization, serving as an alternative to unpopular cuts to services or tax hikes. Indiana ranks seventh behind Nevada and much more populous states like New York and Pennsylvania in gaming revenue, with some nineteen million visits to its thirteen casinos creating $2.2 billion in profits. Greater Chicagoland, including the four casinos in nearby Indiana, is now the fourth biggest gambling center in the US.

On board, I climb up another non-working escalator, not surprised that the image on the massive billboards along the Indiana Toll Road—a multi-racial party of trim youthful couples, drinks in hand, gathered around the blackjack table—doesn't quite match the small crowd I find inside Casino 2 of the Majestic Star. I see only a handful of players on the main deck. Here below me, watching the night go by, are two thick-necked white men and their female friends, clad in sweatpants and sitting on stools at an actual blackjack table.

On the second deck, banks of slot machines line the walls with more slots clustered together in circular islands around the floor, easily well over a hundred lit and flashing at different frequencies. Bells, sirens, rings, and sounds of whirling wheels, all computer-generated, seem to come from both those being played and the overwhelming number that are unused. This nightmare of lights and sounds boomerang around the room with the aid of mirrors and polished golden colored chrome railings and light fixtures. To be fair, I am not the intended audience, nor am I in the proper state of mind to appreciate the "fun" of staring into highly manipulative devices programmed to make you believe that the next press of a button will make the night worthwhile.

An older, overweight woman struggles mightily to stand, rolling back and forth in her chair to create momentum so that she can grab hold of her walker, collect her meager winnings, and go back to playing the slots. I need that drink and move toward what appears to be a bar, but there, two older men stare into screens mounted inside the top of the bar. Apparently nowhere is free from those spinning aces and jacks. A woman bartender asks me if I want something, but I see they only have light beer. I mumble something to her about liquor that she can't hear, and wander on in my stupor, stubbornly in search of a serious drink.

With what energy I still have, I make up my mind to try the other casino, Trump's original ferry boat casino, his great promise to the people of Gary, moored on the opposite side of the pier. Inside, I can see what's left of the Trump brand's garish style embossed in the décor and design of Majestic Star 1. Chandeliers hang low from the ceiling, offering more show than light. Golden colored chrome plating gleams from fixtures and baseboards. Adding to the faux luxurious atmosphere are plush pink cushioned chairs and ruby-colored carpets, and a large mirror runs along the back of the bar, making the room appear if not larger then certainly more manic and kaleidoscopic. Though I can clearly see people at the bar with drinks in hand, I'm so exhausted my mind is unable to turn will into action. I can only stand and stare. Finally, I gather my senses and enough energy to push my body back, out of the casino and down the hallway where I wander about lost until I find a door that releases me out into the lakeshore air.

I lean against a chain-link fence blanketed by a canvas to hide the rip-rap shore and thin strip of beach hidden behind it, a few yards below the casino's roofed entrance and driveway. I look for a place to peer through the canvas, but it is too dark to see the beach. But the lake is there—I can smell cool air and sense that unmistakable expanse of space. For a few moments, I listen to the surf, charmed by the elemental sound of tumbling stones in the surf, reminding me of the lake's presence, always there, always ready to enfold us back into its forgiving emptiness. Eventually, I wander back to my hotel room.

Waking up the next morning, surprisingly I feel little soreness or pain, but when I stand up to walk to the bathroom, my legs feel as if weights were attached to them. I walk slowly to a sliding door that opens out onto a three-foot balcony, pull the curtain around my naked body, open the door, and poke my head out into a steamy grey morning.

From this perch, I have a good view of Indiana's infamous industrial shore and the surrounding brownfields and railroad tracks. As I look right and left along the shore and inland back toward the city of East Chicago, I can't say that I recognize much of anything except the casino complex and the long breakwater of Buffington Harbor. To my left and west, across the placid harbor, is the massive Cleveland Cliffs (formerly Arcelor Mittal) steelworks. The rust-red corrugated metal complex is so large that it not only hides the fields of BP's distillery towers I walked through the night before but also erases the entire Chicago skyline. Moored below the gargantuan mill complex is a lake tanker measuring perhaps twelve hundred feet long, and it's but a quarter of the building's length.

To my right, far in the distance around the shore, I can see the smoke-stacks of Gary's US Steel Works; further northeast is another steel complex at Burns Harbor and Michigan City's power plants beyond it. Maybe five hundred feet beyond my hotel, across two sets of railroad tracks and along either side of the pier, is the casino, the two ferry boats I visited last night, with a three-story concrete parking garage attached to a circus tent-like entrance hall.

Below my balcony is a narrow parking lot and service entrance and beyond it, partially obscured by young cottonwood trees and weeds, is the shore and the lake. From here, the lake looks like a watery desert of creosote, a haze of pollution and August heat rising over the water. The water and the surrounding landscape of weedy brownfields and marshlands is entirely unrecognizable. The scene should depress me, but I'm a traveler in this landscape and find it all strangely fascinating precisely because it's unfamiliar. I scan the parking lot, looking for a place along the fence where I might cross over the railroad tracks and out onto the beach.

This strip of beach before me begins at the Majestic Star Casino and parallels the railroad tracks along the shore for maybe half a mile to Indiana's Harbor and East Chicago's marina and its own casino complex at the shoreline, the Ameristar. The beach and the brownfield behind were all part of Buffington Harbor and US Steel's subsidiary, the Portland Cement Company, which was shuttered years ago. Amazingly, adjacent to East Chicago's Marina and Casino, just below the casino's parking garage, I recognize East Chicago's public beach, Jerose Beach, no more than a few hundred feet long. Even without binoculars, I can just make out the white wooden lifeguard platform and a swing set next to a small pavilion. And as one might expect, being surrounded by a toxic landscape, the beach is one of the most polluted beaches on all of the Great Lakes, making the top ten list of America's most toxic beaches according to the National Resources Defense Council. At least there's someplace for those who live nearby to take their kids to play for a while without having to drive twenty miles to the beaches at the Indiana Dunes.

It's nine o'clock by the time I make it out of my room to try again to find something to eat at the casino. I decide to forgo the ridiculous skywalk and take the short driveway over the railroad tracks to the casino, which can't be more than a few hundred feet from the hotel lobby. But just as I reach the tracks, a minibus pulls up beside me, and the driver opens the door. "Do you want a ride, sir?"

Confused, I squint, unable to see the driver's face. Cupping my eyes to shield the morning sun, I ask, "To where?"

"To the casino."

I look back at the hotel and across the two sets of tracks to the casino, politely declining his offer to ferry me over the tracks and the remaining two hundred feet. "It's okay, I'll walk, thanks."

He pauses. Obviously, something is wrong: "Well, we're not supposed to let you."

I can hear in this older Black man's voice that he's just doing his job and probably doesn't give a shit if I crawl over the two sets of tracks. "Well, I'll just walk if it's okay."

He shrugs and closes the door.

Over the tracks, I head straight to the only place I know I can find any breakfast: "Wings N' Things."

So, along with the frisky crowd ready for a few hours of sitting and staring at wheeling symbols of queens, unicorns, hearts, and piles of gold coins, I stand in line for my own pile of golden eggs served in a pool of grease.

I make my way back with little fuss, cross over the tracks, and as I head inside the hotel and pass the reception desk, I decide I might as well check out. I ring the bell on the counter and wait.

A moment later, out comes the same woman I met two days ago when I made my reservation after surveying the route in my car. Her face brightens into a broad smile: "Did you do it?"

Though I recognize her, my mind momentarily goes blank, not because I don't remember, but because I'm suddenly blushing with emotion.

"You're the man who said he was going to walk from Chicago, right?"

"Yeah, it's me, I made it. Can you believe it?"

She smiles just as she did when I confessed to her my intention to walk here from Chicago. She was my witness as I vowed to myself that I would make this pilgrimage. Here she is once more, reminding me. Standing before her, I realize that she and my taxi driver Gabriel are the only people on this earth who know that I have walked thirty-two miles from my apartment to the outskirts of Gary, Indiana.

Then she calls out to someone in the office behind the desk. "Here's this guy I was telling you about, who wanted to walk here from Chicago. He made it."

Out of the office a tall Black woman in a flowery print dress, clipboard in hand, bustles around the desk and extends her hand. I read her official company name tag and title, Head of Housekeeping. She congratulates me, too. Then, to my surprise, she blurts out a warning: "If you're walking, you have to watch out for the police because they gave my boy-friend a ticket. Just for walking over here from the Ameristar."

"What? Where was he walking?" I ask, incredulous.

"Right out here along the railroad track. He works over at the Ameri-star, and he'd missed his bus so he called me to see if he could get a ride home. He thought it was okay, so he just walked on over here. But they stopped him and gave him a ticket. They said he was trespassing and couldn't walk there."

"Show me the path, will you?"

In the short elevator ride and walk to my room, she tells me how dif-ficult public transportation is sometimes for her boyfriend in traveling to and from work at the neighboring casino in East Chicago just across the water at Indiana's Harbor. I open the door to my room and walk toward the balcony, side-stepping the pile of my things spread out on the floor next to my pack. I open the balcony door, assuming she's behind me. But when I look back, she's still standing outside my room in the hall.

"We're not supposed to enter a guest's room unless we get their permis-sion," she explains.

I wave her in and open the curtains and sliding door.

"There's the trail he was walking on, right down there along the rail-road tracks."

Both of us lean out the glass sliding door as she points to the infamous tracks where I was stopped earlier that morning on my way to breakfast.

The trail runs along a fence that holds back the mounding sand from the beach below and follows along the shore. "See, it goes along that fence by the railroad tracks." She traces the trail with her finger along the shore to the Ameristar Casino's parking garage. We look at each other and shake our heads in disbelief.

I thank her, stuff my things in my pack, and instead of heading back out to the road toward Gary, I make up my mind to explore this path to the casino along the shore, even if it means I'll begin the second day head-ing, for a time, in the wrong direction, or getting a ticket from the East Chicago police.

I take the skywalk back to the casino, find the door out as I did the night before, and slip through an opening in the canvas-covered fence. To reach the water, I must step or rather hop from boulder to boulder along riprap that protects the casino complex from the lake. Scanning the beach that heads west toward Indiana's harbor and East Chicago's casino, I see no one. Above the piles of rock, sand has mounded along the fence, and cottonwoods have shot up, effectively shielding the beach from the railroad tracks and the business of gamblers and gambling. And there outside the fence in the young dunes is the forbidden path to the Ameristar Casino. I head to the water's edge.

It's not the act of trespassing that invites me to explore these kinds of hidden landscapes. Such edgelands offer a feeling of refuge in ways that so-called wilderness zones, left relatively undisturbed by humans, don't or perhaps can't. These are the places I've retreated to since boyhood—paths into empty lots, abandoned houses, alleyways, railroad tracks, graveyards. In these liminal spaces, the land reveals a counternarrative to the ordered world we've learned to admire. Here, nature startles rather than soothes. Here, to our surprise, freedom is not a reward—it is a sensation.

As elsewhere along my shoreline pilgrimage, clumps of marram grass have sunk their roots into the growing piles of sand and littered soil, slowly fulfilling their roles in the natural process of dune-building as they establish the fertility that will allow other plants and creatures to follow.

A sign turned away from me is planted on a post near the fence. Ominously, the yellow color looks familiar to those I've seen at contaminated brownfields and federal Superfund sites. I can't read it from here, so I get out my binoculars. It reads:

CAUTION:

Hazardous Materials Present at this Site

Unauthorized People Stay Out

Out of habit, I step to the surf and kneel to touch the water, gauging its temperature, getting a sense of its swimmable qualities. I scan the serene sheet of golden water before me, looking out as far as I can into the steamy haze along the horizon. Five minutes is all it would take, I think, to strip down to my tights, slip in, swim out a few hundred feet and back—but I remember that I've another thirty miles ahead of me.

My fingers, though, reach through the watery lens, tantalized by the magnified lake stones just below the surface. Over the years, I've become a collector of these miniatures of the lake's geologic story. I've lined my windowsills with them and made piles of them on my wooden porch, among my potted plants. Though their polish and brilliance fade out of the water, their ephemeral color brings delight. Here is a fine assortment: leathery cherts, oval bloodstones, granites of rose and moss, nuggets of pearl-colored quartz, wafers of dark grey slate, and my favorite—the charcoal basalts. The feel of them between finger and thumb, smooth and stone round, their weight lying in the center of the palm, makes me wonder if, when holding stones, what we feel is not the stone in our hand but rather the reverse—the stone holding us.

Among these lake agates there are recent creations of the industrial age, too: the rounded conglomerates of cement and gravel, the meteorite-like slag from the mills, the bricks eroded into salmon-colored soap bar shapes. I collect these, too. Scientists and academics tell us we've left the era of the "entirely recent," the Holocene, for that of the Anthropocene, "the era of the human." The evidence, in the miles behind and before me, is hard to ignore—and it includes the disposable plastics that have piled up on this beach. Like the old stones, the bricks and plastics, the carbonized bits of slag, glass chips, oxidized iron nails, and metals old and newly made, human waste becomes just another layer of the story of the planet. From the perspective of geological history, the fumes and factories of the industrial age are but waves on the lake, cresting then breaking onto shore, leaving a faint imprint in the sand.

If I scoop up a handful of sand, among the ancient broken-down boulders of eras long ago I can see bits of green and blue, yellow and red, white and black, beads of plastic from a more recent era—they've been broken down by the elements too, but within my own lifetime. With a powerful magnifying-glass I'd be able to see microbeads from soaps, solvents and a myriad of plastics used for just about everything we consume.

Here laid out before me on this forbidden shoreline, untouched and well-preserved, is quite the collection of urban detritus. The standard set of plastic trash, faded only slightly by the sun and days or months or years floating in the lake. If you take notice or take it upon yourself to try to remove some, it seems to multiply before you. You lean over and pick up an errant plastic bottle at your feet and magically before your eyes appear two or three more. You pick them up and more cry out. The beach is flooded with the stuff: tampon dispensers, caps and lids, pens, lighters, straws, cups, cutlery. Among the water bottles and usual assortment of flotsam are a less usual scattering of objects the lake spat back onto shore: a high-heeled shoe, a poker chip, a toy football, a plastic champagne glass, a two-gallon container for gasoline, a knotted cord of plastic rope, a buoy the size of my leg, and so on. The plastic trash I see strewn here and everywhere collects in my mind. It isn't recycled. It compounds. It feeds my apocalyptic fears and apoplectic rage at all who can't see what I see in each piece of plastic.

Tossed from cruise boats and pleasure craft, left along the beach, blown in from highways and landfills, flushed down toilets and released by overburdened city sanitation systems along with rainwater, this is the trash Lake Michigan swallows and disperses to its hundreds of miles of shore. Each broken-down fragment, each cup, each spoon, syringe, doll, and rubber glove had a human hand, a use, and a purpose. Each seeming piece of antimatter found and unfound has a history.

Among all of that which has been heaved up onto shore, no bit of flotsam tells the tale of what it means to live in a disposable world better than balloons. Balloons, of course, wreak havoc on birds and fish all over the world, most disturbingly in the oceans, where they can be found in the stomachs of shorebirds and whales and large mammals along with other plastic trash. Researchers at the Rochester Institute of Technology estimate that nearly 22 million tons of plastics yearly makes its way into the Great Lakes.

No matter where you walk on the beaches of Chicago and around the lake, especially to the east into Indiana and Michigan, balloons fly and float onto sandy shores. I see them here as I do now everywhere it seems. Each has a story tied to its colorful ribbon, threaded through the fingers of a particular hand. They carry with them anonymous emotions, afterglows of intimacies: a blooming love, a new baby, a child's birthday, a graduation. Or so we assume when we see them attached to happy people or to the tree in the yard or the hospital bed or even rising free. I did, anyway, until I understood that balloons have other uses, other stories attached to them.

Walking once a few years before along Miller Beach, part of the Indiana Dunes National Park just outside of Gary, I saw so many that I began to count them. When I reached twenty, I got out my camera and documented what I found, curious about why there were so many. I found them in every color, with their matching ribbon tails strung out along the sand or wrapped around bits of wood or caught in the marram grasses up from the beach. On some there were words stamped from the dollar stores and other shops where they were purchased. Some had shapes like hearts. Some were made with a shiny metallic material. Happy faces of sunny yellow. Baby blues. Pink was very popular. Even shriveled, some could still be read. "Happy Birthday," "I Love YOU," "Congratulations!" Some were marked by hand, black markers spelling out a child's name, "K-I-N-E-S-H-A." I knelt before them and photographed each in its natural setting, among other bits of plastics, driftwood, and stones. Some were caught around a dead fish or tangled in the legs of a dead sea gull, attracting insects and flies.

It occurred to me that many of these balloons probably floated across the lake from Chicago—that's why there were so many here, as the winds move generally northwest to southeast, thus pushing detritus to the southern shore of the lake. These prevailing winds have, in fact, formed the dunes themselves, as they sweep sand off the shore and amazingly move hundred-foot mounds of it a bit further inland each year. The same winds also carry tons of toxic pollutants that land primarily on the already devastated communities of Chicago's southeast side and northwest Indiana: Whiting, Hammond, East Chicago, and Gary. The classic downwind calculations about where to build factories follow a pattern across the US. It's not by accident that the wealthy suburbs of Chicago are far to the west and north—and thus upwind—of the industrial corridor of northwest Indiana and southwest Chicago.

I found black balloons, too, that day on the beaches outside Gary. I spotted one lying among the marram grasses in the foredunes, soon to be buried in the moving sands along with the stumps of long-dead black oaks.

Black balloons. Who buys black balloons?

A few weeks after that day walking outside of Gary on Miller Beach, I was watching the local news reporting on yet another shooting of a child in Chicago. There were the familiar interviews with crying parents and outraged neighbors. Then there was another scene, an impromptu ceremony held in an alley. The family and friends stood in a circle, hand in hand, children and adults, surrounding a makeshift shrine of photos, homemade cards, and black balloons, tethered to the ground. At the end of the prayerful ceremony, the mourners let go of each other's hands and each knelt and untied a balloon. One by one the bereaved released the black balloons, symbols of their grief, memorials to another child fallen in Chicago's streets.

Back to East Chicago

From the beach and the casino, an access road leads through brownfields and the ruins of Portland Cement, a ten-story sheet metal structure two city blocks long standing in the middle of acres of weeds. It's the only way to reach the highway and my route ahead to Gary. So, I cross once again—or trespass—over the railroad tracks that parallel the shore. Looking down the tracks I can see that it might be possible to follow them, illegally of course, perhaps to the gates of US Steel through more brownfields, but there on the tracks sits a pick-up with its lights on, no doubt railroad or casino security.

Beyond the hotel's parking lot, which is nearly 90 percent empty, is the enormous parking lot that was to accommodate Trump's planned casino and entertainment complex along this shore. But as is clear from even Google Maps, this lot of several acres has only added to the landscape of toxic ruins along Indiana's shore. The lot is slowly being overtaken by weeds and small trees sprouting through the cracks. The giant parking lot was to be for Trump's fifteen-story hotel, his entertainment hall for prize-fights and concerts, and his ferry boat casinos. But instead here we have aluminum light poles with lamps hanging limply, never lit, and placards identifying the lots for the hundreds of visitors who will never park in Lot A. As I cut through the lot to reach the access road, I stop and take a photograph of the latest in a long history of littered remains left by America's wealthy with their big plans for the people who live along the coast of Chicago.

It begins to drizzle. Traffic is heavy along this entrance road. The road out passes under a railroad viaduct, made decades ago for perhaps only one lane of vehicles. It wouldn't be much of a problem if traffic was light and if it wasn't raining. But a line of cars has queued on the opposite side of this concrete bunker–like viaduct. I could climb over, but there's a fence. Water has pooled under this bridge and cars are moving slowly as they pass through. I wait, thinking I'll have a chance to dash down and through to the other side, but it's too risky. Nobody pays the slightest attention to me standing by the side of the road wearing my baby blue poncho. I decide to see if I can shimmy along a shelf of concrete along the underpass. I make it, though I'm splashed consistently by cars barreling through on their way to their morning fun sitting at the slot machines.

On the other side of the bridge, there is no place to walk except in soggy grass. Here, to hide the abandoned cement complex, the parking lot, and the toxic brownfields, the casino has planted flower beds and a wall of blue spruce and fir trees. Finally, I reach the highway, but not before passing under a metal sculptural banner that reads in cursive lettering "MAJESTIC" with a large star dotting the J. And next to it, easily missed on the roadside, a small sign reminds those who might have missed the bus that, indeed, "PEDESTRIAN TRAFFIC [IS] PROHIBITED."

Across the highway, a few hundred feet inland, the elevated Cline Avenue Expressway passes over East Chicago's industrial lakefront. I head to the underpass to take cover from the rain. There, I notice that on the other side of the expressway is a Speedway gas station fused with America's oldest hamburger chain, White Castle. I've barely walked half a mile and it's already close to eleven o'clock, but I convince myself that I deserve a decent cup of coffee.

With my coffee and chocolate doughnut, I sit by a window on the White Castle side and watch the world before me on a Wednesday morning on the outskirts of East Chicago. By each pump, a man, nozzle in hand, stands staring out at the drizzling rain and the traffic along the Cline Avenue overpass. Inside, a line forms in front of a turbaned South Asian clerk in his thick glass cubicle. The customers point to their brand of cigarettes, recite their lucky lotto numbers, and pay for their gas and salty snacks.

I sip my coffee, content in my role as traveler, observing for the sake of observing as you do when you're on the road and have nowhere to be but where you are.

Workers come and go in their trucks, old and young, keys jangling from their belt loops, soiled work masks dangling from their necks, soot on their shirts and thick arms. Men in boots, men in uniforms, men in hats. Men Black, men white, men brown.

Though I've been in and out of convenience stores with gas pumps since they replaced filling stations, I look around as if I'm a visitor from a foreign country. Taking my time I notice just how much stuff can be sold in a place like this and marvel at the choices and the ease at which we consume on the fly: dispensers with sixteen spigots for soft drinks, three levels of burners for coffee pots, machines for smoothies, slushes, teas, and flavored coffees; floor-to-ceiling refrigerated cases on three walls, shelf upon shelf, full of bottles and plastics of more of your favorites. A dizzying assortment of products, processed, packaged, and displayed for fingers to find and purchase within seconds. All designed so we don't have to ever stop moving.

Midday traffic is heavy on Cline Avenue. From where I sit, I can see only the top halves of vehicles as they travel over the concrete arc of the overpass. Semitrucks embossed with corporate brands, one after the other, carrying their cargo cross-country. At times, the highway appears more like a conveyer belt as thick coils of steel, gleaming tanks of chemicals, crates, and containers trundle along overhead. Since I've been momentarily freed from the tyranny of daily mental habits, things that before I would have ignored in this industrial landscape become curious patterns and structures with histories and consequences that reveal as much about the world I live in as any other selected set of phenomena.

How easily the mind can make the familiar disappear. Why travel great distances if the mundane before you can crystalize and open the doors of perception in just the same way as the new and unfamiliar?

You'd think that gas would be a bit cheaper for people who live in the shadows of one of the world's largest oil refineries. But even though ten-thousand-gallon storage tanks of unleaded gas cast shadows onto your children's swing set in the backyard, that doesn't guarantee that you'll pay any less than people a thousand miles away. Premium, as the sign says on the corner, still is nearly four dollars a gallon, and good old regular unleaded is conveniently priced fifty cents cheaper.

A couple passes my window, plastic bags hanging from their hands. Instead of ambling over to a parked car, they walk through the lot and head out into the drizzle down the road. Inspired, I take their cue, pick up a sports drink for later, pay with my card, and fly out behind them in my blue poncho.

I watch them navigate the puddles along the side of the road, cross to the median, avoiding the potholes, and make a quick move to the other side. All without stopping—they seem to know just where to step and when to cross before the oncoming traffic, moving just fast enough to arrive without having to rush. They walk with an air of nonchalance, giving little hint of fear. I follow their lead until a van shoots a wave of water across my path, forcing me into the soggy weeds. Then the couple turns, crosses under the Cline Avenue overpass, and heads toward Gary.

Here along the road is a newer housing development of modern split-level homes that reflect the economic diversity of East Chicago. As with all of these industrial cities in Indiana that I'm passing through, despite their struggles, there are many middle-class neighborhoods and redeveloped sections that are thriving.

At the light on the corner, I wait to cross. Looking up I realize I'm on the same road as I was on the night before, Columbus Drive, though here it's been updated to honor East Chicago's growing Latino population and is called Cesar Chavez Drive. In the light of day, I can see that if I'd walked a mile or so further, I would have been able to make it to the casino unassisted. Across the road, next to the city's new municipal building and police department, a ten-foot fence surrounds several acres that appear to be original wetlands. Looking a bit more carefully I can see that there's a gravel track just inside the fence. Is this a park? But then I see the corporate logo of Cleveland Cliffs encircled by shrubbery, flowers, and non-native evergreens. The sign answers my curiosity: the green grounds and the handsome new building inside the fence are those of a research facility. The track apparently is for the steel giant's employees to use for recreation.

I follow the walkers under the Cline Avenue expressway as they turn onto the road that will take me into the city of Gary. As they lead the way from the edge of East Chicago back into the brownfields by the lake, I wonder why they're on foot. Has their car broken down? As I follow them, I begin to suspect that this convenience store we've just left might be the nearest source for groceries for those without transport in the nearby neighborhoods of East Chicago or for those who live down the road in Gary. In fact, as I've read, Gary has no major supermarket chain in its city limits. Of course, there are dollar stores here and there. But little fresh food can be found at these stores or at convenient stores. But a city of some eighty thousand without a single major supermarket? This means that those without cars must either take the bus to shop outside the city or walk to a convenience store. Here is a classic example of a "food desert," and how they affect people's health.

A road sign reminds me that I'm walking on US 12, one of America's oldest continental highways, beginning on the shores of Lake Erie in Detroit and ending on the Pacific Coast in Bellingham, Washington. The Old Chicago Road, as it once was called. Essentially, I've been on it or near it since the beginning of my walk. US 12 intersects with not one but two of America's great old highways: US 20, America's longest highway which goes coast to coast; and Route 66, which begins on Michigan Avenue in Chicago, though it has been obscured by the development of Chicago's expressways. Once through Gary, US 12 changes to reflect the more touristic landscape and becomes "The Dunes Highway," but on this stretch from the state line to Gary, it goes by the banal but apt "Industrial Highway."

The rain has stopped, and I have a wide, puddle-free gravel berm. Before me for the first time since I began my pilgrimage the sky is relatively

free of man-made structures, except for a crane-like steel tower in a scrap yard I can see a few hundred yards ahead and that cream-colored band of concrete in the far distance, the Indiana Toll Road.

I've entered the edgelands of Northwest Indiana, a stretch along Lake Michigan's coastline of some six or seven miles that spreads several miles inland in places, expanding in the past decades into urban corridors and neighborhoods in Gary as nature absorbs what humans have abandoned. Between industrial fiefdoms and plundered lands are a mix of toxic waste sites, hybrid cattail marshlands, and former and active landfills. Among slag piles, scrap yards, and fly-ash heaps are historic dumps where a who's who of Chicago's well-respected businesses, medical facilities, institutions, and universities (including the University of Chicago and Northwestern University) for years quietly disposed of their poisons and toxic waste. This area, surrounding the Calumet River system on both sides of the border, has slowly been transformed from one of the largest expanses of wetlands in the United States to a "lost marsh," as the city of Hammond has dubbed its restored golf course. Waste, of course, is a business, legal or illegal.

Industrial Highway to Gary/Chicago International Airport

From the tollway at seventy miles per hour, this no-man's-land outside of Chicago remains a blur of cattails, abandoned buildings, brownfields, swampy thicket, and cottonwood. From the ground, I feel as if I've discovered an unexplored territory where one could spend days tramping about without seeing a soul except for railroad security guards or trespassing birders. How can so much land so close to a city—lakeshore no less: wetlands and groves of trees, forgotten dunes and swales—remain mostly off-limits or erased from the public's imagination?

The first time I recall passing through this landscape was in the early sixties traveling on a family vacation. For a boy used to farmland and small towns, the sight of Gary and East Chicago's steel mills with their fiery stacks and plumes of smoke side by side with Standard Oil of Indiana's fields of flaming cokers and maze of pipelines was utterly mesmerizing. The scene of smoke and fire followed by the railroads, iron bridges, and the towers of Chicago pumped up my father, and as my sisters and

I stared out the windows of our station wagon, his voice would change to the one he used in prayer before meals. For my father's generation, the mills and burning skies along the shores of Lake Michigan were symbols of America's greatness and power, its progress and ever-booming prosperity. These were icons of a sort, monuments, no less potent than civic buildings.

Here and there along the berm of the highway, sprays of sturdy buttery sunflowers sprout from seeds carried by bird droppings and the wind. Indigo buntings sing from electrical wires and goldfinches dip and disappear into the stands of hybrid cattail and weedy brownfields.

The road is nearly empty except for a few semitrucks that pull out from the depot of Swift Trucking Company, a major cross-country carrier. Glancing over into the gravel parking lot, a row of truck cabs gleam, the midday sun catching their chrome grills so that they disappear into a blinding whiteness before my eyes. My fellow walkers have quickened their pace and have left me far behind. I watch them until they become indistinguishable from the highway as it bends, crosses the Grand Calumet, and is swallowed by a thicket of trees along the river.

On the other side of the road, a plywood fence runs several hundred feet along the highway, shielding a scrap yard. But behind a stand of dusty, diseased-looking Chinese Elms in front of the fence, I can see a working conveyor belt as it slowly elevates what looks like a car fender up and up until it tumbles off, falling presumably into a hidden pile of scrap below.

As a kid I spent hours wandering among the alleys and in the rubbish left behind by factories and businesses along the highway that passed through the south side of Marion, Indiana, where I grew up. Just a few hours' drive from here to the southeast through farmland, my hometown, like so many across the upper Midwest, was part of the great industrial supply chain, producing and processing one part or another for Chicago or Detroit with Northwest Indiana's steel. I collected junk and scavenged like an old man, believing I'd come upon some old book worth thousands, or I'd fuse together radio tubes and broken clocks into imaginary machines that could detect signals from outer space. Inevitably, the day came when my father announced he was going to the dump, and out went my collection of gadgets with the empty paint cans and old lumber. But I didn't mind, as no place was more fascinating than our town dump, just outside the city limits by the Mississinewa River.

Pile upon pile of possessions, shorn of their owners and purposes, lay exposed to the elements and the animals that hunted there. Naked bed springs, tongue-splayed boots, bottles of medicines, legless chairs, soiled shirts, record discs, TV sets, and mirrors, all among sacks and sacks of filth teeming with flies. The veil on the ordered world of my Midwestern small factory town was drawn back, revealing a truth—everything eventually becomes trash, ruined beyond repair, and ends up in heaps buried at the dump or in the landfill outside of town. Old men were always there, sorting and stacking this and that item of supposed value, mostly things made of metal. They'd pack their finds with care, tying each bicycle and curtain rod to the jumble atop the beds of their sagging pick-ups. These men were of the tribe of tinkers who scoured and scavenged, holders of unusual powers—or so a boy of ten like me imagined. Arbiters of an object's worth, they were able to resurrect or condemn with a touch of the hand.

Industrial Highway has a newer name here—Airport Highway—though that hasn't helped Gary get its airport off the ground. Here is another large empty parking lot in front of a handsome, relatively new terminal. The sordid, sad story of the opening and closing and opening and closing again of Gary's airport is just another of the political half-measures and grand schemes that have plagued this industrial corridor since the steel industry's downsizing and automation. Empowerment zones, baseball parks, casinos, outlet malls, convention centers, entertainment parks, and most recently, the hope for a Michael Jackson Museum and Performing Arts center—all have, in the end, done little to reverse Gary's precipitous slide. The dreams of turning Gary's airport into a third Chicago hub to relieve traffic at O'Hare and Midway have come and gone more than once. The people of Gary wait, like they have for nearly three decades, for the jobs and the desperately needed tax revenues that an airport could bring to the city, while the power brokers consider who will ultimately profit. For years it seemed a win-win, as Chicago needed a third airport to deal with its heavy volume of flights, but amid political battles between Springfield, Chicago, Indianapolis, and Washington, Gary's airport remains closed to commercial flights, with only private jets, military transport planes, and shipping services making use of the facility. For now. But the plans continue to stir hope.

Behind the airport I can see cranes dredging marshlands along the Grand Calumet, a reclamation project to clean up toxins that have seeped into the river for years. On the other side of the highway, there are the telltale white pipes and fencing of not one but two Superfund sites, Med Co 1 and Med Co 2. Along with Love Canal in New York and my own hometown dump in Marion, Indiana, Med Co 1 and 2 are notoriously recognized as being on the first list of Superfund sites. CER-CLA (the Comprehensive Environmental Response, Compensation, and Liability Act), otherwise known as Superfund, was enacted by Congress on December 11, 1980. The act specifically levies taxes on businesses responsible for the degradation of lands and dumping of chemical or toxic waste that affect or threaten to affect public health or the environment. However, due to the powerful oil lobby, the law does not apply to oil companies. Here, on this stretch of land across from Gary's airport, which itself was built on top of a landfill, the Midwest Solvent Company buried some 80,000 barrels of toxic waste in excavated sand pits. The site was closed after an enormous explosion shot oil drums hundreds of feet into the air, injuring several Gary firemen as they tried to put out the flames and unleashing toxic fumes that reached west Gary. As is so often the case with Superfund sites, the damage to the land, nearby residents, and workers was so costly that Midwest Solvent filed for bankruptcy and the long-term cleanup has fallen on taxpayers. As if these lands weren't eerie enough, next to the superfund sites and across the street from the dormant airfields I pass what appears to be a company that makes concrete vaults of some kind. I peer inside a garage where, from floor to ceiling, stacks of burial vaults await purchase and their eventual and eternal owner.

Across from the entrance to Gary's airport I stop in front of a brown, weather-beaten sign, folding in on itself and about to fall, advertising "Roast Beef Sandwiches," as far as I can tell. No restaurant, no name, no direction. Behind it, a potholed side road leads off to a row of wooden houses with cars in various stages of disrepair in front them, and on the other side, hidden by a stand of trees, I can just make out three abandoned houses.

Ever since leaving Chicago's lakefront, I have found myself noticing these wooden two-stories more and more, not so much because of their ruined condition as because their architecture speaks to me in meanings and memories I had believed no longer held any value. No matter how much these houses have withstood the weathering of time and poverty, in them I keep finding some remaining feature that calls forth whole passages and periods in my life. In the metal porch awnings, the iron railings running down the crumbling concrete steps, the overgrown rose of Sharon next to the rotting roof, the sagging laundry wires, the narrow upstairs bathroom window, I see houses like those in which I once lived here on this highway staring back at me.

These homes, garages, backyards, and streets I pass, first in Chicago and now in the outskirts of Gary, speak to me of my uncles and aunts, my grandparents, my pals and their parents, all the people who made me: the schoolteachers, the nurses, the postal workers, the people of the second shift and time-and-a-half on Sundays. These houses line the roads from here to Erie, west to California, and south to Tennessee. To ignore them as they fall and fold back into the earth—as if they are no more than rotten wood and plaster, blight and broken windows; as if they prove some economic theory or the certitudes of the armchair experts in the media—is to fail to see that each home, each shop, each farmhouse and barn holds an individual past and part of our collective history.

I'm curious what the newish terminal looks like, so I walk through the empty parking lot. I've barely reached the sidewalk in front of the terminal when a tall, stout Gary police officer opens a large glass door, sticks his head out, and startles me: "This place is off limits. What are you doing here?"

I should have expected this confrontation, as right there in plain daylight, twenty-five yards away, sits a Gary squad car, the only car in the lot. Gary's police force, like those in so many cities with skeletal funding, must not only deal with all the social ills that accompany chronic poverty and high unemployment but also try to protect the large number of shuttered public and private buildings. Gary's buildings are prime targets for thieves armed not with guns but with blow torches, crowbars, and wrenches as they scavenge for copper, brass, aluminum, and other metal they can pry loose in the form of fixtures, pipes, or ductwork to salvage for cash at nearby scrap yards.

I fumble out a lie to the Black officer, telling him I'm a journalist from Chicago and want to "talk to somebody about the airport," even pulling out my narrow reporter's notebook from my pack. He relaxes, points me in the direction of a set of sheet metal barracks-like buildings next to a hangar I passed walking in from the highway.

I make a half-assed attempt at checking the office he suggested, feeling his eyes on me as I walk over. I knock, look around, and then glance back across the parking lot, wondering if the officer is watching me. I knock again. No one answers. Why I don't just continue on my way, I don't know. But I push open the door and enter, announcing myself, "Hello? . . . Hello?" The lights are on, screen savers bounce across sleeping screens, there's candy in a jar on a counter. Apparently, they're all at lunch. I pick up a glossy magazine that touts Northwest Indiana's booming business climate, help myself to some candy from the jar, and head back into the heat.

My fears of finding the officer parked outside the door are unfounded, but I nervously hustle back to the road, glancing back at the terminal for good measure. I'm ready to cross the highway when a black Labrador bolts toward me from the woods across the highway, barking ferociously but stopping at the edge of the road.

This is no dog off his leash at the dog park on the lakefront, and it's not happy with this two-legged stranger walking through his turf.

I freeze, with one foot planted on the road. Exposing its teeth, the dog bounces with each hurling volley of barks. A mature male, this dog surely would outrun me in seconds. But where can I go? Back to the office? To the cop in the terminal? Panic, as it will, amplifies the barking, tenses my muscles to the point that I barely can keep my balance. My legs begin to shake. Desperately, while keeping my eye on the dog, I slowly sink down so that I can find something on the ground to hurl if it attacks me. Feeling about, my hands find little more than bits of plastic trash and not a stone bigger than a pebble. Finally, my fingers clutch a dirt clod the size of a golf ball, and I slowly duck walk backwards, keeping one hand free so I don't fall. A car approaches. Quickly I stand, raise my arm to signal, but the car passes without noticing. Angling away from the highway, still scouring the ground for a more lethal weapon, I have an idea. The dog continues to bounce on its feet and bark, creeping along with me on the other side of the road, though stopping every few seconds to take care of an itch.

Across the highway, just ahead on the dog's side, is a side road that leads toward a lime plant on the shore. But on the corner is a godsend—CT's Adult Bookstore.[3]

---

3   CT's Adult Book store has since this walk been demolished.

If the dog stays where he is and I can make it further down the road, I could make a run for the bookstore. When the dog breaks into another scratching fit, I get my chance and make a beeline across the road to CT's.

With my pack slipping off my shoulders from the run, I dash across CT's parking lot and stumble into the bookstore's front entrance, quickly backing up against the door. But the dog has turned around, interested in something else, slinking back into the woods. Placing my hands on the door, I try to catch my breath but as I heave and cough, nervous laughter takes over.

So here I am, standing in front of the plywood door of a former gas station turned into the proverbial, windowless house of sin at the edge of town. My laughter is not so much a nervous response to the dog as it is my wonder at how my path has led to an adult bookstore across the street from a shuttered airport surrounded by Superfund sites and scrap yards. But my pilgrimage has led to this door, and if I've learned anything so far, it's to not ask why but just trust the path before me and all that it presents. So I open the door.

Immediately I'm thrust into such darkness in contrast to the midday sunlight that I can't see much except for a Coke machine to my right. But then the dim décor slowly comes into view. Three white women, wearing tight fitting short shorts, legs crossed, and smoking cigarettes, sit on stools at a bar made of plywood. Another woman stands behind it, having come out from behind a makeshift plywood wall or hallway. Now I can make out the pole. For dancing, of course. To my right, there is seating for the show—a large vinyl couch, a few chairs, and a table. The room, the ladies, and the bar are all lit with bluish light with a lot of help from the Coke machine. I take another step in. But before I can make out much more, a short white guy with an unbuttoned shirt steps out of a tight office next to the door. "Can I help you, my friend?"

"Ah, yeah, maybe you can help me." Thinking fast, I remember that somewhere behind this adult bookstore and the scrapyard down the road, there's a nature preserve I've tramped through a few times. "I'm looking for this . . . nature preserve. Isn't there one around here somewhere? I think it's called something like Clark and Prairie or something like that? It's down this road, toward the lime plant. Right? You know where it is?"

"What? Nature preserve? That's a dump back there. I've never even been back there, man. Nature preserve? Why you want to know?"

"Well, I'm a journalist and I'm . . . "

He cuts me off and opens the door for me to step outside. "Nah, you don't want to go back there." Pausing, he looks around and then back at me, his eyes narrowing as they drill into mine. "You got any protection, man?"

Instinctively, I look back at the police car across the road at the terminal. *Protection?* He'd obviously not witnessed from inside his six-foot-by-four-foot office my dash across the highway to save my skin from that dog. The thought comes to me that I do have a Swiss Army knife in my pack.

But he isn't interested in my answer, he's interested in who I say I am, a journalist. And off he goes on a fifteen-minute harangue about anything and everything, one rage feeding another as he riffs on the airport, Chicago politics, Gary, and "the Blacks."

His opinions have him so excited that before I know it, he's re-enacting a scene in which he caught a Black guy trying to break into a patron's car in the parking lot where we're standing. "He's standing right about where you are, man, and when he made like he was gonna run, I shot the son-of-a-bitch." Then, for effect, he flips open his unbuttoned shirt and pats a large, black revolver, holstered with straps around his shoulder.

As he carries on with his performance, telling me about how the police laughed and dragged the real or imagined thief away in their squad car, I begin to wonder if fighting off that black lab might have been a safer option than talking to this guy who's making light of blowing away a man, whether the story is true or not. What would his reaction be, I think, if I tell him that not only do I not have protection but I'm on my way, on foot, down the highway into the city he so despises, the city that still lives with the notorious title others gave it back in the 1980s: "Murder Capital of America." Gary indeed had the highest homicide rate for a city its size in the 1980s, and over the years has continued to suffer from high rates of violent crime and murder. Obama's 2009 stimulus package helped a lot—before it, Gary's Police Department had only ten working squad cars.

Before I consider making another run for it, he runs out of venom. And as he goes back inside, I march my ass as quickly as it will go down the highway, where the road turns and crosses over the Grand Calumet River, leading into Gary.

Grand Calumet River to Gary City Center

Once again, I cross over another of the Calumet region's notorious polluted waterways—the Grand Calumet, not to be confused with the Calumet, the Little Calumet, or the Indiana Canal. Walking through this industrial landscape of Indiana and Illinois has finally straightened out for me the nomenclature and directional flow of the much abused and confusing system of waterways from which this part of Indiana gets its nickname—"The Region"; that is, the Calumet Region. The Grand Calumet River runs through Gary and meanders through the brownfields, landfills, and hybrid-cattail-choked wetlands I've just walked through, and then a good portion of it drains back into Lake Michigan via the highly toxic Indiana Canal while the rest empties back into the Calumet River.

Like the Chicago River, the Grand Calumet's directional flow has been reversed, although not because of any concern for human health as was the case in Chicago but rather as part of the general manipulation of landscape and waterways to benefit industry. In fact, US Steel moved the river and filled in a mile-wide floodplain when constructing its port and steelworks. As I walk over the river, I can see in the distance Gary's Waste and Sanitation Facility, just one of the municipal waste facilities on the southern shores of Lake Michigan that struggle to keep polluted runoff and untreated waste from draining into the lake, particularly during heavy rains.

If you look at a map you will see that Gary sits on the southernmost tip of Lake Michigan. Over ten thousand years ago, as the Wisconsin glacier receded and ancient Lake Chicago shrank, the southern shore became largely wetlands with swamps and dunes intermixed. In the nineteenth century, after the fur trade wiped out the beaver and mink, early settlers passed over this wild landscape for lands further west that were easier to farm. This began to change with the introduction of the railroad, and as Chicago became a nexus for trade, industrial development followed, and the wild and seemingly worthless dunes and swamps became prime real estate for sand mining, oil refining, tanning, meatpacking, ice-harvesting, manufacturing, and, eventually, steel production.

It takes another mile of patched and pocked highway and steady truck traffic for me to enter Gary proper, but it's hard to tell where what's left of America's last great company town really begins. For over four decades—as Gary's economy has shrunk and its population dispersed—weeds, scrub, and trees have reclaimed roadsides, empty lots, and abandoned businesses. A virtual second-growth forest is returning to some of the city's outlying areas—though Gary only turned one hundred years old in 2006.

The city is named after US Steel's first CEO, J. P. Morgan's pal, the Chicago financier Elbert Henry Gary, whose name also graces another of US Steel's company towns, Gary, West Virginia, a coal-mining town that once served the steel giant but now, too, is impoverished. After J. P. Morgan purchased US Steel from Andrew Carnegie, he purchased land along Indiana's shore, wanting proximity to Chicago's booming economy and access to the lake and to Chicago's rail system. Aware of America's growing labor movement and the powerful trade unions in Chicago, Morgan and his backers specifically recruited foreign workers. What these workers fresh off the boats found wasn't quite the American dream they were promised here along the shores of Lake Michigan. They made this city work, nonetheless.

Wandering among the dunes and what's left of the black oak savannah and wetlands, particularly in and around Gary, I've seen sandpits left by the sand-mining outfits. Many became convenient for dumping slag and other steelmaking byproducts; others were turned into landfills like those I passed a few miles back, where anything and everything was dumped, legally and illegally.

As I round a bend in the road, I notice an oval red sign buried in a thicket to my right. It's so overgrown that the rusted white steel post is almost invisible, so the sign seems to float there silently among the trees. It simply reads SHOPPERS. Other businesses have survived the region's economic decline, and I pass nondescript concrete block structures that have to do with trucking or car repair, construction or security, all well fortified with high chain-link fencing.

Closer to the center of the city, I begin to see a little more life. But not much. Then again, it's mid-afternoon on a hot August day, why would

anyone be outside if they didn't have to be? It's important to remember, too, that Gary is a huge city geographically, at some forty-nine square miles, so its decline and decreasing population density makes it look emptier as well. With over seven thousand homes abandoned or left vacant (it was even higher not long ago, but many are finally being demolished), Gary is among a handful of American cities with a more than 20 percent vacancy rate for single-family residences. Like other struggling rust belt cities, including my own hometown of Marion, Gary has tried to give away some of these houses to residents, offering them the chance to purchase abandoned homes for as little as a dollar in the hope that residents can help stabilize their own neighborhoods while making some money. But it's hard to imagine someone spending thousands of dollars rehabbing a home to sell or rent as long as Gary's population continues to decline and its housing market remains relatively stagnant.

And yet, as I turn down Fifth Avenue, there are the familiar worker cottages along with other small squat brick homes where life goes on. Someone's working on a car in a driveway; in back is the grill with the staked tomatoes next to the garage; there are the roses on the lattice climbing along the house. Across this wide avenue, though, are tar-shingled two-stories that have burned down or been boarded up. Then down another block are the remnants of a row of architectural classics: two-story, stucco, worker cottages, six or eight altogether, some empty, some occupied.

I realize as I continue walking into the center of the city that I'm likely seeing Gary's worst side; as with so many other Midwestern cities, its downtown has emptied out with business closures. I know I could be led—as I have been before, by activists and professors or civic and religious leaders—through other parts of Gary that could show me a whole other city of thriving community gardens, vibrant old and new businesses, renovated schools, and institutions like Indiana University's Gary campus.

Over the years, I've met many people from Gary, white and Black. Like all of us who grew up in rustbelt cities in their heyday of the fifties and sixties, they have fond memories of this city—but when you ask them about the present, they are either bitter or simply shake their heads, unable to explain exactly how it came to this. Gary was also home to the Nobel Prize–winning economist Joseph Stiglitz, who grew up here in the late fifties. "When I was growing up in Gary during its own smog-choked 'golden age,'" Stiglitz writes, "it was impossible to see where the city was going. We didn't know, or talk, about the deindustrialization of America, which was about to occur. I didn't realize, in other words, the rather grim reality I was leaving behind."[4]

On a map it looks like Gary is on the shores of Lake Michigan, like Chicago and Milwaukee, but industry dominates Indiana's lakeshore and nowhere more completely than the seven-mile stretch owned by US Steel's Gary Works. You could live in Gary all your life and never actually see or put your foot into Lake Michigan—as is unfortunately the case for some, particularly children. Gary sits a good two miles inland, separated from the lake not only by the massive mill complex but also by multiple rail lines and the elevated concrete ribbon and major truck route, the Indiana Toll Road.

---

4   Joseph Stiglitz, "The Myth of America's Golden Age: What Growing Up in Gary, Indiana Taught Me about Inequality," *Politico*, July/August 2014). Watching the effects of globalization on America's rust belt cities like his hometown, Stiglitz became so troubled that he devoted his career to challenging economic doctrines of neoliberalism and how they were consolidating wealth in fewer and fewer hands at the expense of working-class Americans.

Two major streets define this T-shaped city: Fifth Avenue, or the Dunes Highway (US 20 and US 12), which runs parallel to the Lake; and Broadway, which heads south from the cluster of municipal buildings where these two once-thriving avenues meet. Along these streets you can see the remains of department stores, post offices, banks, offices, apartment buildings, theaters, churches, shops, and businesses in various states of ruin.

As I walk down Fifth Avenue, I pass apartment buildings built in the thirties and forties that would be prized properties in my neighborhood in Chicago. Some remain unchanged, while others have been completely overtaken by ivy and weeds, with sprouting trees of heaven and Chinese elms creating a wall of growth around the ruins. I stop and stand for a moment before a rusted fence that encloses a football field with a black oval cinder track around it. On the far side, where fans sat behind the home team; all that's left of the old stands are the concrete studs that held up wooden bleachers. Like other schools in Gary, Horace Mann High School, once as big as many small colleges and famous for its progressive curriculum, shut its doors years ago.

Growing up in Indiana in the 1960s and '70s, my main image of Gary was of the towering mills, but coming from another factory town, I accepted these as facts of life. Working factories meant jobs—jobs for uncles and neighbors, jobs that helped me pay for college, jobs my high school friends gladly took and kept until the jobs were gone. My other image of Gary had to do with basketball. Gary's high school teams—and East Chicago's, for that matter—were for a time the envy of every school and town in a state that found in high school basketball a unifying pastime for its disparate regional cultures from south to north. I remember how my father, a high school basketball coach, marveled at the way Gary's teams, composed of almost all Black players, had altered the game, transforming it from a rigid half-court game to one that incorporated speed and athleticism—the full court game that it is today.

Walking down Fifth Avenue in the middle of a Wednesday afternoon, I am mostly alone; here a woman and her daughter get out of a car to go into a clinic, there a forty-something man rides by on a boy's bicycle and pulls into the liquor store down the block.

After the decline of the steel industry in the early seventies, Gary took on a mythic infamy and stigma, changing dramatically from the center of

Indiana's working class "Region" of second- and third-generation Catholic immigrants, largely from Eastern and Southern Europe, to America's largest Black city with its own Black major, Richard Hatcher. In 1968, Hatcher's election in Gary and that of Stokely Carmichael (a.k.a. Kwame Ture) two weeks later in Cleveland stunned the political establishment and terrified white people in those cities and around the country, fueling the fears that initiated the massive exodus of whites out of urban America. Consequently, as the general economic collapse of the region took hold, producing massive unemployment and shocking rates of crime, Gary became the butt of jokes and racial slurs. Thinly veiled cracks about Gary's pollution, once a sign of progress, became codes for Gary's Blackness and justifications for how "they" had brought on the city's devastating decline. Forgotten, however, is how little the state did to ameliorate the declines in its manufacturing cities like Gary. In contrast, the state provided generous tax breaks to Gary's businesses to relocate in nearby Merrillville, outside of the city.

As I walk, I think about how powerful and pernicious these racial codes are in everyday American life, knowing how instinctively they can sharpen into emotional reactions. Why wouldn't someone walking through Gary imagine or see how it is making strides to recover? Or imagine it as Richard Hatcher once did, or as the poet Amiri Baraka did when he spoke before the first American Black National Political convention, held down the street at Gary Roosevelt High School in 1972? "Rise up, rise up, the revolution has come!" Baraka chanted in front of the thousands who came from across America to organize Black leaders, educators, artists, and activists into a potent political force to demand and orchestrate social and economic change. Not surprisingly, the agenda from Gary's historic convention is almost verbatim what Black activists and leaders are still calling for today, fifty years later: economic equality, access to health care, better schools, environmental justice, and an end to racial profiling, police brutality, and racist practices by banks and lending institutions.

Gary was featured in the 2009 History Channel documentary series *Life After People*, in which filmmakers used time-lapse photography to dramatize how quickly nature moves in to fill the void. While it focuses on the biological decomposition of abandoned structures, the documentary also reveals the incremental effects of environmental degradation on the health, economies, and futures of people caught in the epicenter of a slow-motion disaster. In Gary, environmental destruction is an ongoing event that has lasted for decades now. Day by day, year by year, the effects of poverty and toxic environments take their toll not only on physical and psychological health but also on the health of the social networks and public institutions all cities need to function. The environmental writer Rob Nixon has described this incremental process of ruin on the environments of the poor throughout the world as "slow violence." And it's an apt description of much of what I've seen since I left the Lakefront Trail.

Across the street, long shuttered, is the shell of a mom-and-pop grocery that reminds me of the corner groceries of Chicago, most run by Latino and South Asian immigrants, as well as those of my youth before convenience stores and pharmacy chains proliferated. On the outside by the door, homemade signage advertises the common staples. And walking across the street to get a better look, I can see hand-painted outlines of various items and black uneven script under each: a loaf of "bread," a quart of "milk," a "soda" bottle, and a pack of "cigs"—all these products seem to dance there along the grey plastered wall below the boarded-over window. In the weedy, gravel parking lot on the street corner stands an old Bell Telephone box with its receiver left dangling off the hook.

The glare of the midday sun washes out what little color there is left in this city. Of course, there's a Walgreens and a McDonalds, and the usual cell phone shops and cash exchanges. With cruel irony, one of the newest buildings on this strip is a freshly minted branch of Chase Bank, J. P. Morgan's presence still hanging on.

Like those of Detroit, Gary's ruins have been well documented by photographers. One infamous landmark still stands on the next corner, just off Fifth Avenue—the gothic Methodist Church, once filled on Sundays with the city's white-collar middle class. I walk half a block down a side street to look and stop before a wrought iron gate. Trees with trunks the size of my arms have taken over the courtyard, spreading so that it's hard to see the well-made brownstone structure with its spire, vaulted doorways, and windows, some still with stained glass.

I can see that a side door to the church has been permanently pried open, so I push through part of the fence and stand in the courtyard. The spire and part of the roof have fallen in. In the miniature forest in the courtyard, I spot an empty bird's nest at eye level a few feet away. I slowly make my way to the door and peer in. Light pours through the breached ceiling. Inside, I step over clothes, trash, fallen plaster, and debris. Clearly the church has been used as a shelter, with evidence of a fire, fast-food packaging, and opened cans. Down a doorway that leads to a basement, I see a little stage and piles of what look like choir robes. In the sanctuary, there's more rubbish—shattered pews, ceiling beams, plaster from the fallen roof. Water pools on the floor from the rain this morning. A sparrow flies out through the opened roof.

Surrounded by stone and trees, the sanctuary is a relief from the heat, though the air is dank and gives me a nauseating chill. Outside the church, however, and across the street, children play, awaiting parents who've just arrived to pick them up at the new single-story charter school with a red and white banner which reads, "Excellence Begins Here!"

I walk to the center of Gary, passing its tallest building, the Centier Bank, the former Gary State Bank building, rising ten stories over the city, a bulwark of brick and steel to showcase the city's role in erecting a new America of industry and technology. I can see the hospital a few blocks down on Broadway, and like in many struggling cities, it now is a major employer.

Here, at the intersection of Broadway and Fifth, the city remains relatively intact except for a stone shell that once was its post office. Two handsome gold domes house municipal and county offices, and next to them is the tired-looking Genesis Convention Center, where residents gathered to say goodbye to Gary's favorite son, the King of Pop, Michael Jackson. In the cluster of buildings that harbors what remains of downtown are the police station, various clinics, and a large single-story mortuary covered in an industrial-looking aluminum siding and surrounded by a large asphalt parking lot. Among these buildings at Gary's center is a small plaza surrounded by angled parking, with planters and some benches. In the middle of it, I come across a statue. It does not honor J. P. Morgan or Elbert Gary, but rather it is a depiction of three giant steelworkers, ten feet tall, cast in steel (of course), shoveling coal and working with molten metal pouring from a cauldron. With grimacing faces and tight jaws, these thick-bodied figures honor those workers who literally built this city as well as forged the steel that built cities across the country.

The humidity and heat drive me inside a sandwich shop across the street from another of Gary's schemes to salvage something of its lost downtown business district—a forty-five-million-dollar minor league baseball park, The Steelyard, home of the triple-A South Shore Railcats. Entering the new-looking sandwich shop, I pass a young Black man in a chef's hat sitting in the shade by the door. Both the parking lot and the restaurant are empty. As I walk in, he follows, calling out to his co-worker, and a smiling young Black woman comes out from the back.

There aren't a lot of choices, but I'm just glad to be in air conditioning and ask her what she recommends. "You want the catfish sandwich? You get fries and a drink?"

She hands me a 24-ounce cup, and I hobble over to the soft-drink dispenser and fill it up with Mountain Dew, drink half, and fill it again, this time adding Pepsi, so eager to get fluids that I don't care which lever I pull. I sit down at one of the twenty or so empty tables and stare out the floor-to-ceiling windows, dazed and dripping in sweat, watching a group of children run across the wide street, balloons in one hand and large plastic bags with some local bank's name on it in the other, presumably holding goodies. They've come from the ballpark, where I can see two white women escorting more Black children and their mothers out to the street.

A day for the kids at the empty ballpark, a chance to play and run freely on the only field of grass anywhere near downtown.

Sitting here in the cool air behind glass watching children happy with their day in downtown Gary, I feel a sense of relief. I've made it nearly fifty miles from my apartment door. I've passed through cities and neighborhoods feared and forgotten, through fenced lands of steel structures full of machines and robots, lands devoid of human life save for those who maintain security and monitor production. I've passed through dystopian landscapes defiled by dumping, environmental devastation, and economic disaster. But my body hasn't given out. My legs and feet are sore but functioning. No one except a dog has tried to stop me.

In Gary, the land and its living inhabitants go on despite the turning away of so many levels of society and governance. It isn't only my own past that Gary evokes for me but the past that's a part of everything stretching in all directions. What is done here is done there: a wound in the body of one man leaves scars on all who live around him.

The two teenagers go to work on my order. I stare out the window at the heat and the empty stadium. No one else comes in. When my food arrives, a spoonful of cold slaw, a pile of long limp oily fries, two slices of white bread, and enough fried catfish for two more sandwiches, I eat as much as I can, wishing I could somehow eat enough to compensate for the missing customers and everything else that has gone missing from Gary, Indiana.

East Side Gary to Miller Beach

I trudge on out of town, passing several rusting sheet-metal warehouses with adjacent fenced-in stockpiles of steel bars and girders stacked and sorted by size. Next to the warehouses, piles of tar-black railroad ties fill several weedy acres. In the US, trains keep our cities and factories aglow and then take away our toxic trash and scrap destined for China or elsewhere so that it can be reborn into something new for us to buy next year. Not long ago, these cities in Northwest Indiana were at the center of America's railroad nexus along with Chicago, not only because they crisscrossed this landscape but also because factories here forged the rails, made the engines, and built the cars that hauled fresh meat as well as the lords and ladies of America's aristocracy.

Another quarter mile brings me to what was once one of Gary's middle-class neighborhoods on the outskirts of the city. I can see two- and three-story wooden homes along tree-lined brick streets like those of the nicer neighborhoods I knew growing up in central Indiana. Here, too, the homes once had substantial, stately porches with stone steps. But now they're worn and weathered, weary with weight, as if they themselves had witnessed a slow disaster and shared the pain of the people who'd lived inside them.

Standing alone on the road, I discover another of the city's municipal ruins, a single-story stone library that once served this community. The stone facade has a handsome portico of faux pillars and three large stone slabs as steps that lead to a solid wooden door. The roof must have collapsed years ago. Two shady maples stand in front. I walk up to the steps and study a carved limestone frieze maybe six feet long and three feet wide that graces a panel parallel to the door. The stonework reveals craftsmanship of another era. The sculpted scene depicts an older man with a beard sitting before a fire with a cup that he is passing to a younger man sitting across from him. Above the two figures a stylized sun shines with a book at its center. Below them it reads: "Knowledge Is Power." The cup, like the book above radiating from the center of the sun, represents the realm of knowledge, an invitation to read, learn, and thrive. Another panel has fallen off the building and lies in a pile of rubble covered in thick, tall grass.

Making my way to the edge of town, I come upon a life-sized crucifix, weathered and dark, made of wood and mounted on a pedestal. It stands alone in a triangular lot along the highway, facing those driving into the city from the northeast. I don't see any visible script or scripture. I guess that the lot and statuary are part of a park. But why a crucifix was placed here is a mystery to me as an outsider.[5] As I pass the trees and the dark figure of the body of Christ nailed to the wooden cross, I start to turn back to take in its full effect from the front—but then I stop, something in

---

5   It turns out that there is an elaborate story and legal history to this particular crucifix, part of a display of crucifixes around Northwest Indiana at prominent locations, purportedly to honor veterans. This crucifix and one built in East Chicago became the subject of years of legal battles between the Knights of Columbus who erected the crucifixes and the local chapter of the Indiana Civil Liberties Union. Eventually, the ICLU won an injunction in federal court to have the crucifix in East Chicago removed as a violation of the Separation of Church and State clause of the US Constitution. The Gary Crucifix remains as legal efforts have stalled.

me refusing to acknowledge such a symbol, on the outskirts of a city that needs no reminders about the meaning of sacrifice.

Further from town, I walk by a couple of ramshackle wooden buildings. One has a wooden sign in the shape of a large six-foot-tall ice cream cone tacked to its front, its yellow color fading to grey. The carry-out liquor store next door still seems to be in business. Once known as the "Gateway to the Dunes," the Dunes Highway thrived with tourist attractions, motels, and vacation homes, but when Interstate 94 was built to the east in the 1950s and the steel industry downsized, traffic and customers with money went elsewhere.

Past this block, the wetlands and woodlands return. Off to the left is one last, crumbling urban street with another row of graying wooden homes slowly being overtaken by entropy. When I reach the opposite corner, it looks as if someone had thrown out a whole bag of colorful trash. But it isn't trash. It's a pile of weathered teddy bears, purple and lime green, florescent pink and brown. As in Chicago, a street corner is the place for a shrine to the latest neighbor lost to the vagaries of urban violence. Here it appears that the victim was young. The balloons no doubt shrunk weeks ago, but they're still here along with the photos and folded notes of goodbye.

My thoughts are shattered by the oncoming South Shore commuter train, sucking all the sound out of the air. I turn from the wet teddy bears to look at the train as it disappears down the tracks beside me. Making multiple daily trips from Michigan Avenue in the Loop to South Bend with speed and electrical efficiency, the South Shore is the last of Indiana's once expansive system of interurban trains that connected scores of towns big and small, taking people to work and sewing the state together in ways that are unimaginable today. It will be my ride back if I make it.

In the distance, I now get a fuller view of Gary's steelworks along the lake as the Indiana Toll Road descends from its concrete stilts and swings east. From my perspective a good two or more miles away, the size of this mammoth mill can only be gauged by geographical features of similar stature that one might find in the Midwest. River bluffs come to mind, or the glacial oddities—the kames and eskers—that rise out of the farmlands of southern Wisconsin. I suppose, if I'd ever seen them, I could compare the steelworks to the two-hundred-foot grand central dunes of Indiana's shore, but they were bulldozed before I had the chance.

I watch a billowing cloud of steam and smoke rise from the twenty-five-story chimneys, a cloud two or three times the size of the mills themselves, so large it's visible not only from Chicago but also from the wealthy shores of Wilmette and Lake Forest further north. Out of view are the slag hills and coal mountains, the coke and scrap metal piles—and between them, still standing, a sand dune with its unusual fauna that are found together nowhere else on earth but along this shore. If I were in a plane above this wall of industrial architecture, I'd be able to see the transformed shoreline, the half-mile long breakers and the port of Gary, one of the largest on all the Great Lakes, built solely to serve US Steel. As with Indiana's Port not far away down the shore, not only did wetlands have to be destroyed and dunes bulldozed, but nearly eleven million cubic tons of sand had to be removed from the shore.

Though trucks have been passing me all day, once I'm outside of Gary the trucks seem more plentiful and annoying. The force of each truck sucks me into its wake, making me move well off into the trash-laden weeds. I've been on the sides of highways before and know what it feels like when trucks blow by at 65 miles-per-hour. Like a large breaking wave, the force of both the air and the decibels of sound coming from sixty tons of hurtling cargo and a roaring diesel engine shake not only me but also the ground under my feet. Finally, in a fit of rage, I scream as the next truck passes, its wake of fumes and dust covering me as I search on the ground to find something to hurl at it. What has come over me? What must this sound do to the health and sanity of those who live nearby? Hour upon hour, day upon day, year upon year?

Where are these trucks going? Some turn onto the tollway, but many are coming from or going to the Port of Indiana a few miles ahead, which keeps these roads busy day and night with trucks, hundreds of thousands every year. On top of the heavy industry and the power plants, those who live along the shore in industrial Indiana must also live with the exhaust from one of America's major transport routes. Two of the country's largest trucking firms, XPO Logistics and Knight-Swift, have major depots outside of Gary. And Gary, like other struggling cities, was grateful to have them, regardless of what came with them. The trucking business is booming at well over seven hundred billion dollars annually. With more and more goods coming from Asia and the explosion of online shopping, 70 percent of the cargo that moves across the US travels on roads and expressways. Traveling through this industrial corridor, a motorist might think the worst polluters were BP or the many steel mills or power plants, but their own cars and all the trucks they're passing account for their share of soot, dust, and carbon dioxide, presenting serious public health problems for those most vulnerable to poor air quality: infants, children, older adults, and pregnant women.

As if to answer anyone who doubts these insidious effects, a monumental billboard rises out of the weeds for those who live in this industrial region to consider: "CANCER" it yells out in bold six-foot-tall lettering, and underneath, in equally loud lettering, "LYMPHOMA?" Accompanying these ads for law firms along the expressways is always a stern but handsome white male face, a hero ready to come to your legal rescue with big dollar promises to compensate for a husband's lost income, a child's lost mother.

Leaving the post-industrial landscape of Gary, I notice that from time to time I suddenly seem able to see with much more clarity and intensity some feature before me in the landscape. For example, seeing a red-winged blackbird flying against a backdrop of electrical lines somehow illuminates for me that thin yellow stripe buried under its wing. I look out into the distance over the lake and notice the shapes of clouds. I find myself staring intently at roadside trash. I feel compelled to catalog it in my mind. Like an archeologist, I study what's come to rest on the road from those who have passed this way before me. Why so many cups and cans and bottles? Why children's shoes, single gloves, t-shirts, underwear, and hats? Why whole bags of discarded fast-food containers, cardboard boxes, cigarette butts, lighters, tubing, condoms, bricks, broken CDs, toy balls? Why so many plastic bags? Why so few newspapers, paperbacks, or pens?

When I reach the concrete pillars that hold up the tollway, the litter stands out even more, perhaps because there's more of it and no weeds to cover it. Tires, tire rims, tools, bolts, springs, and other mysterious metals from a million machines with wheels rolling by. Did it come from above, falling off trucks and cars, bouncing down from this elevated river of traffic?

Under the overpass I find piles of rubble, scrap lumber, buckets, and paint cans leftover from construction work. And yet there's life here under this bridge. In fine dust turned soft by the rain from the night before, I see hundreds of imprints left by the feet of pigeons that take shelter and nest here in this artificial concrete cave.

With relief I turn off the highway onto an angling street through Gary's Aetna neighborhood, which borders the beginnings of the Indiana Dunes National Park and the beach community of Miller. Small, wooden one-story houses, set well back, line the street, shaded by native cottonwoods and black oak. Here I find a sidewalk, partially covered under creeping weeds, litter, and grass clippings. To my surprise, along the edge of the walk is a prickly pear cactus, its splayed dusty green pads with their distinctive purplish buds lying on the concrete. Kneeling before it, I touch its barbs, a reminder of this plant's remarkable biological story. Though now more familiar in the American Southwest, the prickly pear is a traveler from ages past that found a home in this northern desert along the shores of Lake Michigan. Seeing it, I know I've arrived at what's left of Indiana's forty-some miles of coastal dunes.

V

THE INDIANA DUNES

There is no inner man, man is in the world, and only in the world
does he know himself.

—MAURICE MERLEAU-PONTY

Miller Beach to West Beach, Indiana Dunes National Park

Leaving behind the highway, I cross the South Shore and commercial rail tracks and enter Miller Beach, Gary's far northeastern neighborhood, the only part of the city that rests on the shores of Lake Michigan. At last, after some thirty miles, I can breathe, and my eyes are free from the sight of oppressive smokestacks and steel structures and the destructive swath they've left behind along Lake Michigan from Chicago to Gary.

Looking at Miller's historic city hall before me, a three-story block of red brick, erected next to the railroad, I imagine how this landscape might have once looked a hundred and fifty years ago, when this landscape of swamps and wetlands paralleled the woodlands and rolling dunes along the Lake. The town of Miller was but an outpost along the railroad lines heading into Chicago, like so many others around the city. With these lands around Miller preserved as parklands, the story of the land and the people who've made it their home feels more present. Or has walking itself sharpened the lens of history, inviting me to see much more than just what appears on the surface?

Before J. P. Morgan and US Steel built their steelworks and the company town of Gary, Swedes had settled here to farm and fish, later harvesting ice in the nearby lagoons when Chicago's meatpackers learned how to refrigerate railcars.

Eventually this lakeside community became Gary's most affluent neighborhood as the city grew to be Indiana's second most populous city by the late 1950s. Along with white collar executives from the steelworks, Gary's Jewish community flocked to the area. Close to Chicago, this beach community among the dunes also attracted a bohemian culture of artists, writers, gays and lesbians, and scholars.

As I walk down Lake Street, Miller's main street, I see small businesses and eateries on both sides. Here are renovated storefronts, a pizza place, a cultural center, restaurants and bars, and a new bank, as well as the shuttered small businesses and empty lots. There was hope that when the Dunes National Lakeshore expanded, essentially surrounding the neighborhood, Miller would again attract tourists and Chicagoans, as it did when it was a summer retreat for artists and writers like Nelson Algren. Despite the trails, lagoons, and beaches, however, US Steel still looms over the western horizon, as does Gary's economic stagnation, making even creative urban pioneers hold back. Gary's renaissance may be slow and come in fits and starts, but as I walk on, I can see there are seeds here in this diverse and historic community that are blooming.

Though the National Park Service has a few short trails and an environmental center for school groups here, this westernmost section of the park attracts far fewer visitors than the other sections up the coast. This part of Indiana's dunes was saved from intense sand mining, and consequently, though the area is circumscribed by US Steel on one side and railroads and neighborhoods on the other, there are patches of wilderness here where plants and animals flourish. Urban parks challenge our traditional ideas about what kinds of landscapes should be valued as "nature" and preserved for recreational use. Here there are no monumental redwoods, no waterfalls or rocky peaks. But what has survived, thanks to chance and the dedication of local citizens over the years, is a window, an extended view outward as well as inward into the natural world that expands when we see it unbounded by our ideas of what it ought to be.

Though I feel heaviness with each step, and the oppressiveness of the afternoon heat weighs on me, I've made it through the industrial corridor and its cities, the longest stretch of this walk, beginning the day before in Chicago's far eastern neighborhood along the Calumet. Though I've hiked in nearby Miller Woods and down to the beach, as I have elsewhere along this pilgrimage, I've not walked into this community and down its streets.

I've often imagined myself living here, believing somehow I might be able to buy a small house. A simple one-story, four rooms, a wooden frame, a slab of concrete in the back, a yard, a garden. It's a fantasy I have allowed myself. What does it mean to have a door of your own out into a community of people that you know, passing neighbors working in their yard or sitting on their porch? Looking around, I wonder what my life might be like here: To be able to wander from my doorstep into a landscape that leads into woodlands and up into these dunes that have been moving inland since the glaciers receded? To wander along a beach, swim when you choose, paddle a kayak into the vast spaces of Lake Michigan or navigate the forgotten waterways that link the wilds of city and nature? Is this why I've come all this way—to convince myself that I belong here—or *somewhere*—before I die?

When I discovered Miller Woods and Beach, I wanted others to share it. This was the place where Nelson Algren and Simone De Beauvoir took refuge from the world to write and walk for miles along the beaches. They are among a long line of writers, artists, scholars, and activists from Chicago and around the Midwest, not to mention those queer and mixed-race couples who for years have found the freedom to create homes among the sand dunes all along this shore into Michigan. Not far away along the shore, Jacques Marquette and his party of French explorers stopped after their successful passage from the Mississippi River. These thick woods and swampy wetlands also served as a major haven for Black slaves as they fled north to Canada. Here, too, the first ecologist in America, Henry Cowles, and his students studied the succession of plants as they rooted along the shore, building the dunes, season by season, attracting other plants, insects, and animals.

And, as if to reinforce their historical importance to both biology and literature, Miller Woods and Beach are home to a rare subspecies of the Karner blue butterfly (Lyceides melissa samuelis) initially discovered by the devoted lepidopterist and literary master Vladimir Nabokov in upstate New York. This is one of the few areas in North America where the Karner

blue can be found, dependent as it is on the wild lupine flower that grows here as well.[1]

Ironically, some of the wildest and most remarkable biodiversity can be found in this corner of the national park alongside US Steel's slag mountains and massive steelworks. I've come across botanists and birders here while walking in Miller Woods and down to the shore. As is the case all along Indiana's shore in places where it has been preserved, here, walking into the thick oak and maple forests, each quarter mile takes you through one dramatic example after another of geographic variations and with them an astonishing diversity of plant life. Eventually you come to one of the lagoons of the Grand Calumet River, serene and empty except for a guy fishing, and on you go over sand hills, through little bluestem and marram grasses, until you arrive at the lake, hardly believing you've traveled through so many ecological communities in little more than an hour.

Now that I've entered the National Park, there are essentially two paths I can take. One follows the beach as far as it goes to the Port of Indiana. The other follows a former railroad bed turned walking trail that passes through the neighborhoods in Miller Beach, past several inland dunes and the park's wetlands, known as the Grand Marsh. Eager to get off asphalt, I opt for the re-purposed railroad bed called the Marquette Trail. But first, knowing that this will be my last chance to eat anything, I turn off Lake Street and find an old gas station structurally unchanged from the 1960s just a few hundred feet from the trail.

A South Asian American couple runs this outpost. Business is brisk with people buying gas at the four pumps and milling about in the repurposed repair garage that's now a tiny convenience store with the usual overpriced grocery items, drinks, and snacks. The woman in a lovely scarlet sari seems completely out of place behind her wall of yellowed bulletproof plastic. I feel a bit embarrassed unfolding my damp five-dollar bill and placing it in the metal tray for her to finger and fold into her register.

Outside, I sit on the concrete curb, savor the sweet scent and taste of an ice cream sandwich, and watch the after-work traffic returning home to a much different city than the one I passed through two hours before.

---

1   Unfortunately, naturalists have not spotted the rare species in the park in the last few years and fear that due to climate change and decreasing habitat the butterfly may never return.

When I get up, my body reminds me of all the work it's done in the last thirty-plus hours on this adventure along the shore. My first steps down the sidewalk are shaky. A car full of male teenagers, sound system at full volume, booms by me, and immediately I feel my muscles stiffen, wondering irrationally if they'd yelled something at me.

The entrance to the trail lies just ahead, and I climb—or rather hobble—up a wooden ramp. I try to rationalize with myself as I hurry along on the soft sand to reach what I've waited for all day, the shade of the dunes' old black oaks. Already soaked in sweat, I feel it trickling down the back of my neck. Now that I'm on a somewhat secluded path, I should feel at ease without the noise and the traffic, but instead I feel strangely vulnerable walking alone.

To my left, below, through the trees, I see backyards, swing sets, wooden decks, kiddy pools. Someone's mowing their yard. I'm not alone but rather still very much in the suburban community of Miller Beach. Then down the trail comes a jogger, an athletic Black man, maybe forty, running at a casual pace. His presence immediately defuses my fears, and as he passes, I catch his eyes and nod. In them, and in his whole body, I see something of my own reflection. They reveal, not surprisingly, his own anxiety about discovering me—a nervous-looking, disheveled white hiker walking with a limp through his neighborhood.

More black oaks and wild grape vine engulf the trail, hushing the sounds of trucks on the highway and the city not far away. Mosquitoes swarm around me. The trail dips and rises as it circumnavigates the inland dunes, and in the depressions, I see swampy pools surrounded by verdant stands of cinnamon fern and skunk cabbage.

Ahead, thicket along the trail has been cropped. Then through more woods, the trail opens out into a marsh. Here and there benches invite people to sit and scan the water and wildlife. Except for the electrical lines in the far distance and another railroad on the other side of the marsh, this is the first vista of land relatively free of human alteration that I've seen in two days. Whether because of dehydration, extreme fatigue, or my heightened emotional state, I'm not sure, but as I stand there absorbed by what's before me, my legs begin to tremble, sending a tremor through my weary body.

I've been ahead of myself much of the day, eager to make time, eager to make it through Gary, rushing, checking the time, my eyes straining to take me forward. From years of practice living with the intense ups and downs that accompany depression and a chronic, life-threatening disease such as HIV, I have learned to redirect my mind away from the physical and psychological effects of emotions. To a fault, of course. Eventually, though, the emotional body has its way.

I imagined there would be some reflective moment toward the end of my walk if I made it. Some recognition of how far I've walked, looking back across the lake from the dunes. Some enhanced perspective on the effects of industrialization on the environment and communities living in the ruins of capitalism. But I didn't expect any revelations.

As is so often the case with travel, though, the body seems to journey on a separate path from the one planned by the mind.

And what has my body gleaned from these sixty miles it has plodded over? What impressions has it absorbed that might guide me in the days ahead back in the daily routines of my city life, circling the same streets and floors of my third-story flat? What does the body know that it needs to honor? Faith, it says, have faith in what lies below, for it is all that we have and all that we are, no more, no less. Feel it, know it, care for it, die for it.

What have I been walking on for the last two days but a vast wetland intermingled with dunes? Savannah lands of oak, prairie, and shallow lakes used to ring the entire southern shore of Lake Michigan. Only today, after all this walking, have I finally reached what's left of this massive filtering system—the part of it that hasn't been drained or so severely poisoned as to be turned into a permanent toxic waste site.

Carl Sandburg called the dunes of Indiana and southern Michigan our Midwestern Grand Canyon. These defiantly wild wetlands and sculptured sand dunes along the great waters of Lake Michigan could temper our hubris and remind us that we are beholden to the elemental forces that brought life from the mire and muck. That is the poetry here: to be stopped in one's tracks and feel one's feet held up by sand blown from the bottom of the lake—and to know that one's own shaking flesh is made from the selfsame stuff.

Exhausted, I could sit here and watch the sun go down, the herons hiding in the sedge grasses and red-winged blackbirds balancing on the cattails. I hadn't bargained for this cumulative effect of wild beauty defined by rust and ragweed, flora and fauna indifferent to the mess of human history. I'm under the influence of that spell called gratitude. With fumbling hands, I pull off my pack to find my field glasses.

Just as I put down my pack, a sound from behind startles me. I step back with alarm and turn around in one motion. Three white-tailed deer have crept down a small dune covered in thicket and trees to browse along the shore of the marsh. They've caught me unawares, shaky, out of my element, walking alone in what's left of theirs.

Slowly, I turn away from the family of deer and back to the marsh, raising my binoculars back to my eyes. Adjusting my lens, I spot a green heron, its shape-shifting body shrinking as it senses my presence. The heron's neck and bill form a statuesque facsimile of the cattail nearby. From a silhouette I pick out a snowy egret in the far distance among some mallards, that curve of its neck embedded in my memory from watching its relative, the cattle egret, riding the bony cattle of West Africa. As I scan the banks of the marsh, a great blue heron emerges from the linear foliage of reeds and grasses, and as usual, spotting one brings another into focus, and another, as the eye learns to distinguish the shape from its surroundings. These winged creatures are reminders that in our manufactured landscape there persists a prehistoric order of things that does not show up on our maps. They are hopeful creatures that way, and when I see great blue herons floating over the city, I follow them, grateful for the suspension from my scripted day, watching their long wings work as they fly from the Chicago River to a retention pond along the highway.

As often happens with binoculars, the narrow focus makes me appreciate the wider lens of my own eyes, and I must put them down to feel that momentary sensation when the eyes are once again free to be absorbed by what they fancy. In this case, it's the light of the late afternoon sky amplified by its reflection in the open water.

A train crosses on the other side of the marsh, a slow rolling string of coal cars, coming from behind one stand of oaks and disappearing behind another. Each railcar is tagged from top to bottom in bold colors and stylized letters, one artist's work blending into another in an organic mash-up of raw expression, an unraveling scroll that reads like a musical score singing of life along this rustbelt route.

West Beach to Burns Harbor, Portage, Indiana

From the Great Marsh the trail leads onto a well-surfaced asphalt road that curves around a small dune thickly covered in gnarly black oaks to the entrance to West Beach. Though I've been walking in the park for a while, here is the sign I've been waiting to see, that familiar chocolate-colored wooden sign posted from Acadia to Zion, here to announce this American landmark and its sacred value to the public: "Indiana Dunes National Park." Here, too, is the stamp of the National Park Service, its logo in the shape of an Indian arrowhead with those romantic symbols of nature—snow-covered mountain peaks, a redwood, and a leaping American bison. It's a sign I associate with summer and family camping trips, adventures in the backcountry, and the grand monuments of America's ancient geography, sites sacred to its first peoples.

Here, though, on Indiana's shore are no snow-capped mountains, no towering trees a thousand years old, no wild buffalo anymore—indeed, little grandeur that commonly defines great natural wonders and national treasures. Here, fifty miles outside of Chicago, between steel mills and power plants, cut in half by one of the largest ports on the Great Lakes, hemmed in by railroads and highways, and sharing beaches with gated communities, is one of America's few urban national parks. For over fifty years, through dedicated work by organizations like Save the Dunes and others, rebutting those who thought it a waste of taxpayer money, the park has survived, and it continues to grow acre by acre.

The park mostly parallels the shore and consists of dunes and wetlands, while sections added farther inland protect prairie remnants, a bog, and an historic homestead. Totaling only fifteen thousand acres, it is one of the smallest national parks, and certainly the only one where you can stand on a beach surrounded by wilderness and see a metropolis across the water and tall smokestacks on either side of you down the shore. Once sacred to the Miami and Potawatomi and generations of native peoples before them, the park is more than just beaches along Lake Michigan. It also includes other geographical features of this unique part of North America: here there are bogs, swamps, tall grass prairies, remnants of boreal woodlands, eastern woodlands, lagoons, dunal ponds, fens, and oak savannah, as well as some of the tallest freshwater dunes in the world.

Opening out before me, at last, are the dunes, not as big as those further north, but undulating freely as they have for millennia, the brown sands sprouting the familiar oaks and grasses, the pines holding the crests along the shore. Though I can't see the lake yet, I can feel it just beyond the foredunes.

I walk on down the smoothly surfaced road, past the entrance and gatehouse, ignoring the sign that mentions fees, figuring that someone on foot at this time of day won't need to pay. I don't get far: "Walk-ins must pay a dollar fee, sir," comes a voice from behind me.

Two young park rangers, in their classic brown hats, green pants, and pressed white shirts, huddle by their colleague stationed at the gatehouse.

After fifty-five miles, I have an audience who I'm sure will appreciate my feat. I grin, announcing playfully: "Does it apply for people who've walked here from Chicago?"

Tired from a long hot summer day dealing with the public, they aren't much interested. "Yes. It's a dollar for everyone."

"I really did walk from Chicago."

"It's a dollar," says the ranger from inside, backing up her partner.

Realizing I've not impressed anyone except myself, I fish around inside my pack for a crumbled dollar bill, smile insincerely, hand it over, and walk in.

West Beach is a popular section of the national park in part because it offers all the elements of the park in miniature and has a large parking lot. It's nestled between two beach communities—Miller's Marquette Park and Ogden Dunes, homes hiding in the dunes and behind tall white pines and oaks. Here, the beach is wide, and beachgoers can walk freely for a few miles back to Miller Beach or ahead toward Burns Ditch, where I'm headed. Or they can climb into the surrounding dunes or meander along by the marshlands where I had been walking.

Along the road toward the shore, I can see more prickly pear and other quintessential species of grasses and plants common to the inland dunes: here are wild rye grass and little bluestem, reeds and rushes, sand cherry and dune willows along with the odd flowering spurge and the bladder-worts, all intermingled with the familiar goldenrod and milkweed.

I pass through a large parking lot, drifting sand slowly encroaching around the edges. People are beginning to leave the beach, young couples, young families, brown, Black, and white, mostly locals like me, although almost all of them I would guess will return to their nearby homes and apartments via their cars. Bathers drag their beach chairs back to their cars. Leggy children, towels draped over their tiny bodies, follow reluctantly behind their parents. An organized group of teenagers, boisterous and slaphappy from a day at the beach, reminds me of my own first trip to the dunes in middle school and the role this same trip plays every year for school children across Indiana and Illinois, for many a rare opportunity (maybe their only one) to take in this wilderness of sand and the natural wonder of Lake Michigan.

As I head through the parking lot to the dunes and the beach behind them, I look at the surrounding crests and blowouts, the darkening skeletons of oaks sticking up along with the oddly shaped cedars and stunted pine, the woodlands in the distance. I know where I am now.

West Beach was where I often came to walk those wintry months I volunteered at Indiana's State Prison, just up Highway 12 in Michigan City. When the prison wasn't under a lock down, I spent Fridays with the men and other volunteers practicing the rituals of Zen Buddhism. Under the watchful eye and loaded shot gun of a prison guard, we sat in silence, walked in meditation, chanted the Heart Sutra, and bowed before a ceramic Buddha on a cardboard box. Despite the calming effects of the sangha and the rituals, I left the nineteenth century prison numb in body and soul. Cold from hours sitting on the concrete floor of the dank unheated prison chapel, I would sit in my car, the heater on high, shuddering and sullen, dreading the drive back to Chicago through the very landscape I have just walked. Sometimes we celebrated one of the men taking the Buddhist precepts and receiving his robe, and when we did, we had food and tea, and I'd learn of the men's lives and the landscapes where they had grown up in the Indiana towns I, too, once knew well.

Led here by the prisoners, I found solace next to the mills in these wild hills of sand. The cold air freely blowing off the lake, the sky still but for the sound of the gulls, the lake vast and steel blue with floating chunks of ice. Men who can only watch the skies and stars from their cells—had they sent me here, to do what they could not: walk along a lake that lies within half a mile of the prison gate? Thinking of those men now, here, after walking for two days, I wonder if those visits to the prison to sit and walk in meditation had not in some way led me to make this journey back.

Now I know a bit more clearly why I needed to make my own path back to these dunes that have for so many before me served as a public shrine, giving all who come upon these crests a place to feel held without words, without conditions, as all places of refuge do.

Walking up into the dunes toward the lake, here, as in Chicago, I can feel the presence of others, of the forgotten and of the trailblazers. I think of those first social workers who made treks to the dunes, following their teacher, Jane Addams, who understood the value of recreation for children and adults alike. I think of the story a Latina student of mine once wrote who'd grown up in East Chicago and recalled watching her mother climb up into these dunes, her fists shaking skyward, sobbing in grief for her lost son who'd died as so many have in the mills, sacrificed in the maw of the furnaces.

From the first steps along the sidewalks of Sheridan Road back in Chicago, my mind has meandered off into memories of other trails, other geographies, other adventures here along this lake where I've spent most of my life. The memories have come and gone with no discernible order or meaning other than to remind me that I am who I am because of how these landscapes and experiences within them have influenced not only how I see the physical world but also how I know myself. Indeed, the Nobel Prize–winning physiologist, physician, and philosopher of mind Gerald M. Edelman's adage about perception is true: "Every act of perception is an act of creativity, and every act of memory to some degree is an act of imagination."

I walk up a wide series of wooden steps that climbs over a small dune and down to the beach. A pale orange sky with streaks of soft pink greets me as I make it to the top set of steps. Along the sandy crests the grasses begin to darken in the diminishing daylight. And then, at the very top, at once I feel my heavy legs and fatigue while I look out over the lake to where the underbellies of the clouds meet the water.

Approaching the lake from the backside of the dunes never fails to dramatize the magic of human perception. No matter how many times I've walked up a dune, with my mind fully prepared for the sudden jolt of expansive vision awaiting me at the summit, in the moment of first glimpsing the lake as it fills my entire field of vision I always feel as if I'm seeing it all for the first time. There's this hiccup between seeing and knowing when time feels suspended from units of measurement. It makes me wonder if perception is not so much an act of the embodied mind reading the physical world as it is the physical world electrifying our senses so that we become aware of ourselves, as the French philosopher, Merleau-Ponty proposed in his musings on perception. Merleau-Ponty understood what becomes obvious on a long-distance walk: the body, not just the brain, participates in the ongoing act of perception as one moves through a landscape.

Here and there groupings of children remain engrossed in play, working on their imaginative creations of shaped sand or dancing in the mild surf, while parents lie nearby on their blankets half-buried in sand, arms and legs intertwined, voices low and warm. On beaches we seem to rediscover that we and everyone around us are essentially bodies under our garments, freed at last, released for a while from cultural norms about what they should be, what they should feel, and what they should look like. Barefoot, we become alive to instinct; exposed to the elements, we feel what we are made of—we sink, step by step, into the sand, into the moment, into the place where we are.

A teenage couple walks hand in hand down the steps onto the beach, darkened in silhouette against the setting sun, a young Black man and beside him, a foot smaller, a petite young Latina woman with long black hair, towels draped over their bare shoulders. They walk toward the western glow that for now saturates the industrial horizon in a blaze of color.

I head along the shoreline away from the remaining beachgoers, alone on my path but content to be on the ancient sands among those who savor these open spaces along the shore. Down the beach, a mile or more, I see another set of industrial boxes and smokestacks that lie ahead, and beyond, out of view, there are more still, many more: Cleveland Cliff's second massive mill complex, the Port of Indiana, the coal-burning power plants of Northern Indiana Public Service Company.

If I'd packed a sheet, I could call my pilgrimage complete, climb up into the waves of marram grass or higher up among the ghostly black oaks and few remaining white pines, make a burrow for myself in the sandy slopes, and sleep without fear of the patrolling rangers in their off-road vehicles. I have nothing else to prove. I've walked far enough.

Just before I reach the boundaries of this section of the park and the exclusive beachfront homes of Ogden Dunes, I plop down on a shelf of sand and take off my shoes and socks, my shirt and hiking shorts. I sip on my sugary sports drink, unwrap another power bar, and savor the sensations of my body at rest. Staring out into the deepening blue of the lake, I can feel the heat and humidity of the day in my muscles and in the marrow of my bones and all is of the same matter, the same molecules floating about in space. I see myself naked and swimming in the surf, and the anticipation is sweet.

Glancing to see how far I am from the few left on the beach, I head to the water. With one motion, I step out of my athletic tights, high step it naked through the surf, and dive into the lake.

Once submerged, my flesh and muscles go limp, and rather than take a stroke, I sink in the shallow surf to the sandy bottom, where my pilgrimage began. For a moment, I sit there like a boy, the soft sand giving way to my weight, rooting me in place until a wave lifts me back up. I lean back into a dead man's float, head back, arms out, legs bent, as I learned as a child, my mother's hand holding the small of my back, whispering, coaxing me to relax. It's that time of evening when, though the sun has set, it still hits the distant white buoys as they bob in the warm blue water. The gulls glow, too, their angled wings holding them aloft as they dive for food.

If I were to drift out a few hundred feet more, I could see the dunes in their proper scope and size, as their slopes rise from the shore and appear to be held by the plants and trees that have rooted upon them.

Yet, from the water, it's clear that they are also the creations of the wind and the waves. The dunes here are not as large as those last remaining giants further north, near Michigan City, that tower over the surrounding landscape of forests behind them. Still, as Henry Cowles observed over a century earlier, all along Indiana's shore the dunes stand as living sculptures, demanding that we use our imagination to understand the forces and lifeforms building and rebuilding them day by day before our eyes. The study of natural science is not for the impatient, but if one learns to look carefully and calibrate the imagination to the rhythms of elemental forces, one can understand why scholars and sages in the ancient world based all that they knew on what they learned from studying living creatures and plants, observing the rivers and tides, noting the orbits of the sun and stars.

Refreshed by the water and the short rest, I quickly dress, rise to my feet, and head north down the beach. The sun has set, and the lake is shrinking as the horizon moves toward shore with the disappearing light. As I note this fact, taking in the panoramic sight of lake and sky, dunes and trees, what it foreshadows for the road ahead doesn't alarm me. I rationally understand that I cannot walk the remaining miles in what little light there is left in the day. I know, too, that soon I'll be forced back onto that dreaded Dunes Highway and I'll have to follow it into forested areas that engulf the road. Yes, that map of what lies ahead is there for me to imagine and fear. But from the beginning of this trek along the shore to the dunes, I've been under the influence of the traveler's mind, a state that I refused to relinquish upon my return from the UK, carrying it with me as it had carried me along those craggy wind-swept cliffs on the Isle of Skye and through the moors of Devon. And though I feel the danger of what lies ahead and the risk of pushing my body even further, I'm not about to let go of this state of mind now after it's unveiled to me how estranged a place can become if we believe it's too familiar to explore with our own feet. Besides, in our anxiety of not knowing what lies ahead there can be a revelatory sense of freedom, what the poet John Keats, a long-distance walker himself, aptly expressed as "negative capability." In this state, Keats believed, we feel infused with a sense of confidence that comes from embracing what we cannot control or understand, and in so doing we discover that there is no distance we cannot travel, no boundaries we cannot cross.

With reluctance, I walk on, keeping to the strip of wet sand between the water and the dry beach. Though I try to pick up the pace, knowing how far I have yet to go, my legs have been unharnessed by my swim, and no matter the anxiety finally coming over me now as I gauge the dimming light, they no longer respond with the same alacrity as before. Is it fatigue? Most certainly. After all, those thick quadriceps, and long hamstrings of mine have done the heavy lifting, along with the joints of the knees and hips. So well-designed and honed these legs of mine, these feet that have taken nearly a quarter million steps since I planted them beside my bed the day before and began this walk.

Unlike much of the rest of the shoreline of Lake Michigan outside of public parks, here within the national park those who own property along the shore cannot restrict park-goers from walking along their section of beach, though signs clearly remind you that you've left the park and entered "private property."

In the water, teenagers are racing their plastic kayaks, shouting, and enjoying themselves. Above in the cottages nestled in the dunes, a couple leans together over the railing around their wooden deck. I imagine them having dinner later with their guests, drinks in hand, admiring the glittering skyline of Chicago across the lake.

I envy their views and sandy slopes, their sightings of rare bird species at their feeders, their fires on the beach at night. As I pass residents out for their evening strolls with their happy dogs, I can feel how far away I am from the streets of Gary, though I can still clearly see the darkened rectangular shapes and smokestacks of the mills far down the beach.

Before the dunes had become prized real estate for industrial use and beach communities, this landscape was wild and open for campers, fishermen and hunters, poets and painters, naturalists, and the seekers of solitude. There were no permits, no lots, no lights, just lanterns and fires. They brought their canvas tents or built their simple shacks and spent the summers away from the clamor and smoke of Chicago. Then there were but a few rustic lodges for visitors and only a smattering of permanent private homes and cottages.

Somewhere along this stretch of beach is where the legendary Diana of the Dunes is said to have lived in her abandoned fishermen's shack. Here, the brilliant young student of mathematics spent nearly two years alone, winters as well, in something of a Thoreau-inspired spiritual quest. It's unclear why Alice Gray left the city and her studies at the University of Chicago in the fall of 1915 to live in solitude and simplicity among the dunes, where the few things she owned came from the lake, as she describes in her fragmentary diary: "Everything I have here, the chair, this cap I wear, these tins, are driftwood, drifted in from the lake—I, too, am driftwood." Gray became something of a celebrity when newspapers in Chicago and elsewhere picked up her story, even tramping through the thick woods and marshes to interview her for their reader's titillation, especially as they spread rumors that she sometimes liked to bath nude in the lake and run along the beach to dry herself. Folk mythology keeps her legendary life alive with stories and sightings of ghostly figures floating in the shallows at dusk or running in the surf. Perhaps even more so because of her tragic end. In 1925, in nearby Michigan City, she was beaten to death by her husband, whom she met along these shores.

Having walked all this way, following her path along the shore and in life, from the time we each spent as studious souls at the University of Chicago to our mutual search for solitude in the hills of sand forty miles around the lake, I feel an affinity for her life and quest. She exists now, I think, not as story or legend but rather as a part of this place, alive to all who utter her name, as it evokes not just the wildness of these dunes but the human spirit that, once released, refuses to be bound.

In the fifty-six miles since I've stepped foot out of my apartment, I've walked little more than a mile on the actual and original shore of Lake Michigan. If Henry Cowles and his fellow Chicagoan Steven Mather, the first director of the National Park Service, had succeeded in convincing Congress to establish a National Park along Indiana's shore back in 1915, I would have before me fifteen miles of uninterrupted beach all the way to Michigan City. Twenty continuous miles, in fact, of Indiana's shore would have been preserved as well as thousands more square acres of inland dunes, wetlands, and forests. Instead of the segmented park, the original proposal to establish a Dunes National Park would have created a park free of industrial use with but a few private cottages or lodges. Like the Appalachian Trail, conceived by Benton MacKaye in the same decade as a response to the overcrowding of American eastern cities, Mather, Cowles, Jens Jensen, and others believed the Indiana Dunes could be a refuge for the masses crowding into Chicago and other regional industrial cities. Even Daniel Burnham's "Plan for Chicago" envisioned concentric parks that extended outward from the city and specifically included Indiana's shore and these dunes. Before me, if they'd succeeded, I'd see the grand set of dunes that was to be the heart of the park, as they were the most magnificent in size, towering over the marshes and forests behind them, where hikers could gaze out and on clear days see far along the shore all the way to Wisconsin.

Instead, I face Burns Ditch, dug originally as a drainage ditch for local farms. Now it's a waterway that serves inland residential harbors and a kind of moat that separates recreational lands from Indiana's Port and the industrial complex surrounding it. On the other side of the thirty-foot wide waterway stands US Steel's finishing plant, and in the distance behind it, I can see what looks like sand dunes, but they're giant piles of slag covered in sand. Beyond the slag hills and steel plant is Burns Harbor, Indiana's second port, two quarter-mile-long rectangular slots dug out of what was once the tallest set of dunes on this shore, some nearly two hundred feet, grander than those cherished by millions each year at the Indiana Dunes State Park down the beach.

The giant dunes are gone, along with a large swath of the Great Marsh; instead, here, blocking my path and forcing me back to the highway, are the infamous three miles of shore that were sacrificed in the so-called compromise brokered by President John F. Kennedy that allowed for the creation of this existing Dunes National Park. Defying reason and the passionate pleas of nearby residents and protesters from Chicago and around the country, the state and federal governments decreed that in this three-mile stretch, the wetlands would be drained, the trees felled, the dunes flattened, and the sand bulldozed, sold, and shipped to be used for landfill and construction; a great portion in fact went across the lake to expand Northwestern University's lakefront campus in Evanston. No other possible sites were chosen for the new steel plant—not the defiled lands I walked along earlier, lands already mined and developed and used for dumping, properties largely owned by US Steel and the Railroads. No, Bethlehem Steel had got their way and Indiana got their port.

I've learned over the many years I've come to the dunes, alone or with friends or taking students, that to think of what has been sacrificed is to diminish what remains. And yet I can't erase the history of this lakeshore, so sacred to so many who have dedicated themselves to its study and preservation, aware as they were of its inherent value that would long outlast them. I don't have to close my eyes to see what is no longer here—the grand central dunes of Indiana's shore—I can see them. By walking, I can see them more clearly than ever before.

Due to severe erosion of the lakeshore caused by a number of breakwaters constructed over the years to protect Indiana's port, Cleveland Cliffs steelworks, and other shoreline industries, the beach has almost disappeared here next to Burns Ditch. So, I must climb up onto a shelf of sand and the downward sloping dunes to continue on my path. Meandering on, I walk through a newly built park that gives nearby residents and parkgoers another boat ramp and picnic ground.

Heading out back to the highway, I walk over Burns Ditch on a wooden bridge reinforced with steel. As I cross, I note the pipes that cross over with me, one labeled with the warning: "CAUTION GAS LINES." What's in the other pipes I don't know. On the other side, facing those entering the park by car, I notice this small sign: NO PEDESTRIANS.

Back on the Dunes Highway, where I began the day, I notice gratefully that traffic has thinned. A truck beeps. Red taillights disappear as the road winds down into the woodlands. Then a group of motorbikes honk as they roar past, their lead rider raising his fist, offering what I take as a salute. What I look like to them—a mentally deranged man walking at night along a highway, a religious pilgrim striding across America to save his soul—I don't know, but their acknowledgment lifts my spirit and sagging shoulders.

The sound of my footsteps, the slight crunch of rubber on fine gravel, becomes metronomic and meditative, and as the light retreats behind the sand-covered hills of slag, I just walk.

Acknowledgments

While walking the Camino de Santiago in Spain, I received an email from Amy Farranto, my editor at Northern Illinois University Press. From that day onward, she has kept this book alive. I'm deeply grateful for her patience, guidance, and vision.

I'm indebted to those many friends, students, and family members who over the years have read my work, buoyed my spirits, and kept me writing: Anne Alderfer, Mark Alderfer, Jo Ellen Ash, Nicolas Barron, Eliza Bent, Elizabeth Giarratana Brown, Patrick Carew, Gavin Van Horn, Gerry Gorman, Julie Ann Hill, Sam Love, Joe McCracken, Kathleen Mullaney, Susan Tillet, Vicky Tomko, and Ann Whalen.

Special thanks to:

Ron Engel (author of *Sacred Sands*) and Joan Engel, for their close reading and for setting me on the right path.

Michelle Niemann, editor and environmental writer, for her insight and professional advice.

Tuong Nguyen and his son Jalin Nguyen, for their photographic assistance and support.

Lisa Roberts, for her thoughtful reading and support of this book and for believing, from the beginning, that the walk needed to be chronicled in a hybrid work of nonfiction.

Rob Nixon, mentor and friend, for reading early drafts and helping me visualize the structure and personal voice that I used in this book.

Tim McMains and Zack McCracken, for their long friendship and encouragement, and for graciously offering their home on Waiheke Island in New Zealand as a place of solace and refuge.

And thanks to all those activists committed to the preservation and health of the neighborhoods, cities, and ecological communities I passed through on my way to the Indiana Dunes National Park.

BIBLIOGRAPHY

Addams, Jane. *Twenty Years at Hull House*. New York: Bedford/St. Martins, 2017.

Algren, Nelson. *Chicago: City on the Make*. Chicago: University of Chicago Press, 2001.

Basho, Matsuo. *The Narrow Road to the Deep North and Other Travel Sketches*. Translated from the Japanese by Nobuyuki Yuasa. London: Penguin Classics. 1966.

Burnham, Daniel, and Edward Bennett. *Plan of Chicago*. Centennial Edition. Chicago: Great Books Press, 2009.

Calvino, Italo. *Invisible Cities*. Translated by William Weaver. New York: Harcourt, 1972.

Carson, Rachel. *Silent Spring*. New York: Houghton Mifflin, 1962.

Cassidy, Victor M. *Henry Chandler Cowles: Pioneer Ecologist*. Chicago: Kedzie Sigel Press, 2007.

Cronon, William. *Nature's Metropolis: Chicago and the Great West*. New York: Norton, 1991.

D'Eramo, Marco. *The Pig and the Skyscraper, Chicago: A History of Our Future*. Translated by Graeme Thompson. London: Verso, 2002.

Daniel, Glenda. *Dune Country: A Hiker's Guide to the Indiana Dunes*. Athens: Swallow Press/Ohio University Press, 1984.

Day, Dorothy. *House of Hospitality*. New York: Sheed and Ward, 1939.

De Beauvoir, Simone. *America Day by Day*. Berkeley: University of California Press, 1999.

Dewey, John. *The Philosophy of John Dewey*. 2 Volumes in 1. Chicago: University of Chicago Press, 1981.

Dubkin, Leonard. *My Secret Places: One Man's Love Affair with Nature in the City*. New York: David McKay Co., 1972.

Dyja, Thomas. *The Third Coast: When Chicago Built the American Dream*. New York: Penguin Press, 2013.

Engel, J. Ronald. *Sacred Sands: The Struggle for Community in the Indiana Dunes*. Middleton, CT: Wesleyan Univ. Press, 1983.

Engel, J. Ronald, and Joan Gibb Engel. "The Visitors to the Duneland Studio: Frank V. Dudley and the Early Movement to Save the Indiana Dunes." In *The Indiana Dunes Revealed: The Art of Frank V. Dudley*, edited by James R., Dabbert, pp. 49–77. Brauer Museum of Art, Valparaiso University, 2006.

Farley, Paul, and Michael Symmons Roberts. *Edgelands: Journeys into England's True Wilderness*. London: Jonathan Cape, 2011.

Franklin, Kay, and Norma Schaeffer. *Duel for the Dunes*. Champagne-Urbana: University of Illinois Press, 1983.

Greenberg, Joel, ed. *Of Prairie, Woods, & Water: Two Centuries of Chicago Nature Writing*. Chicago: University of Chicago Press, 2008.

Grossman, James, Ann D. Keating, and Janice L Reiff, eds. *The Encyclopedia of Chicago*. Chicago: University of Chicago Press, 2004.

Heraclitus. *The Collected Wisdom of Heraclitus*. Translated by Brooks Haxton. New York: Penguin, 2001.

Hurley, Andrew. *Environmental Inequalities: Class, Race and Industrial Pollution in Gary, Indiana 1945–1980*. Chapel Hill: University of North Carolina Press, 1995.

Huxley, Aldous. *Brave New World*. New York: Harpers Perennial, 2006.

Jacobs, Jane. *The Death and Life of Great American Cities*. New York: Vintage, 1992.

Keats, John. *Selected Poems and Letters*. Edited by Douglas Bush. Boston: Houghton Mifflin, 1959.

Klinenberg. Eric, *Heat Wave: A Social Autopsy of Disaster in Chicago*. Chicago: University of Chicago Press, 2002.

Love, Samuel, ed. *The Gary Anthology*. Cleveland: Belt Publishing, 2020.

Mabey, Richard. *The Unofficial Countryside*. Stanbridge, Dorset: Little Toller Books, 2010.

Machado, Antonio. *Border of a Dream: Selected Poems of Antonia Machado*. Translated by Willis Barnstone. Port Townsend, WA: Copper Canyon Press, 2004.

Merleau-Ponty, Maurice. *Phenomenology of Perception*. New York: Routledge Classics, 2002.

Miller, Donald. *City of the Century: The Epic of Chicago*. New York: Simon and Schuster, 1996.

Nixon, Robert. *Slow Violence and the Environmentalism of the Poor*. Cambridge, MA: Harvard University Press, 2013.

Sandburg, Carl. *The Chicago Race Riot, July 1919*. New York: Dover, 2013.

Sebald, W. G. *The Rings of Saturn*. Translated by Michael Hulse. New York: New Directions, 1998.

Sinclair, Upton. *The Jungle, A Norton Critical Edition*. Edited by Claire Virginia Eby. New York: Norton, 2003.

Solnit, Rebecca. *Wanderlust: A History of Walking.* New York: Penguin Books, 2001.

Stead, William T. *If Christ Came to Chicago: A Plea for the Union of All Who Love in the Service of All Who Suffer.* Madrid: HardPress Publishing, 2013.

Stiglitz, Joseph. "The Myth of America's Golden Age: What Growing Up in Gary, Indiana Taught Me about Inequality." *Politico,* July/August 2014.

Tuttle, William M. *Race Riot: Chicago in the Red Summer of 1919.* Champagne: University of Illinois Press, 1996.

Whitman, Walt. *The Portable Walt Whitman.* New York: Viking Press, 1974.

Wright, Richard. *Black Boy.* New York: Harper Collins, 2008.

Zenke, Janet Edwards. *Diana of the Dunes: The True Story of Alice Gray.* Charleston, SC: History Press, 2010.

www.ingramcontent.com/pod-product-compliance
Lightning Source LLC
Chambersburg PA
CBHW020606251125
35938CB00022B/527